IGNITE YOUR

SALES

HERO

By James Logan

TABLE OF CONTENTS

Introduction

Embark on a game-changing sales journey where the psychology and mindset behind a successful sales career unfolds. Take a deep dive into insightful sales strategies and unlock the secret sauce and tactics that will empower you to close more deals – a lot more!

This book is not just a guide. It is an indispensable companion for salespeople, sales trainers, sales managers, and business leaders alike. Prepare to maximise your potential as an individual and elevate your organisation to new heights of sales success.

PART 1

A CAREER

IN SALES

It's About the Top Two Inches

———

The best part about embarking on a successful sales career is that there are very few barriers to entry. Practically anyone can get a job in sales and start that journey. It's all about having the right mindset and learning on the job.

As you start mastering the fundamentals of selling, your skills can quickly become transferable and open the door to endless career opportunities, financial rewards, and a lifestyle that others will envy.

The caveat lies in the crucial distinction between simply having a job and building a sustainable and prosperous career in sales.

The top two inches is a common phrase in the sports world meaning mental strength. By gaining a deeper understanding of your own psychological state, you can pinpoint areas for improvement and overcome obstacles, challenges, and limiting beliefs that may be standing between yourself and your desired future.

Chapter One:
Find Your Sales Purpose and Motivation

If you have a passion for sales, the opportunity to build a long-term, successful sales career can be a powerful aspiration. The reality is that while some succeed, many will remain within the same salary range and job type for their entire career.

Just as there's a big gulf between a talented amateur sportsperson and a successful professional, the same applies to a sales career. The difference is that a sales amateur can still make a living, albeit without reaching their potential or enjoying the trappings of sales success.

What separates the talented amateur from the professional is often down to the top two inches, in other words, their mental strength.

In the early stages of any career, we tend to be easily satisfied and set a low bar. There is no obvious reason to start thinking about legacy and what's most important.

As we get older, things change. We start thinking about where we are heading and what our life goals should be. That's why the pathway to a successful sales career is a journey, not a destination.

For example, nothing focusses us more on our values and place in the world than the birth of our first child. This can manifest itself by heightening our resolve. We start thinking about the future. What were previously random thoughts and aspirations can quickly change into something more purposeful.

> What separates the talented amateur from the professional is often down to the top two inches; in other words, their mental strength.

Getting Started

Having a well-defined personal plan or framework to help identify your sales purpose and motivation is a powerful way to either rejuvenate your existing career or get you started on your sales journey. This is distinct from other forms of goal setting as it essentially provides you with a template for steering your sales career in the right direction, while also keeping it real by incorporating your values and life goals into the plan.

Here's how this can work from an individual salesperson's perspective.

Step 1 – Identify your sales purpose.

Identifying your work or career purpose is about aligning your outer life with your inner self. If you have a passion for sales and aspire to a long-term, successful sales career, this aspiration may already be your sales purpose. This is just an example; you may want to be more definitive. However, being more definitive can also be restrictive in the bigger picture.

Step 2 – Identify your core values.

The next step is to identify the core personal values that define who you are. It's not practical to select more than five or six. The idea is to focus on what's most important.

There are countless online databases that can help get you started. Here are some examples of core personal values: gratitude, family, honesty, friendship, respect, open-mindedness, well-being, humility, dependability.

Step 3 – Declare your intentions.

The next step is to declare your sales intentions. By declaring your intentions, you can start synchronising your day-to-day work life in accordance with your sales purpose, beliefs, and values.

It's important to understand that as circumstances change, intentions can also change. You may retain the same purpose and values, but any single event can alter your course of action.

When you first identify and write down your intentions, they may seem vague. If so, you're on the right track, as they're there to provide the pathway, not the detail.

Here are some examples of declaring your sales intentions.

- My intention is to be considered the best regional salesperson in my industry.

- My intention is to use every learning opportunity to become more employable for either my current or future employer(s).

- My intention is to manage my own environment within my employer's business.

- My intention is to provide my family with everything they need, and more.

- My intention is to achieve the perfect balance of work-life harmony.

Now you have identified and stated your sales purpose, values, and intentions, you can use shorter term goal setting to flesh out your intentions and regularly measure the effect of your daily, weekly, and monthly actions.

As an example, a subheading to your intention of achieving the perfect balance of work-life harmony could be to drop off and pick up your children from school at least once a week. Another could be to go to the gym for a workout at least three times a week. Remember, this is about reminding yourself about who you are, not what you want. If you want to be better, then be better.

Developing Your Motivation

Our motivation is the driving force behind our future actions. As an example, the need to provide for our families can be a powerful motivator that gets us out of bed and off to work every morning.

Once you've established your framework, it's time to focus your motivation so you act and behave in a way that keeps you moving in the right direction. It's now about more than getting out of bed just to earn a paycheque.

Types of Motivation

There are two types of motivation, external and internal.

External or extrinsic motivation is generally driven by external recognition and rewards. The easiest example is that we need to work to make money, to survive. Extrinsic motivation is the primary weapon used by sales managers, charged with meeting the revenue expectations of their employers. They motivate their sales teams through offering new learning opportunities, giving positive reinforcement, providing rewards for meeting revenue targets, and finding ways of maintaining interest in activities that can be repetitive and dull.

Internal or intrinsic motivation comes from within us and is driven by internal rewards. An example of intrinsic motivation could be the decision to have a vegan diet. It not only makes us feel good, but also has a higher meaning by aligning with our values and identity. Intrinsic motivation is often attributed to high achievers.

Even fear of failure can be a powerful motivator.

Here are some of the obvious daily differences between a salesperson who is motivated externally and one with internal motivation.

- Motivated by having a job and company car vs motivated by building a career.

- Motivated by office interactions vs motivated by 'flying in formation' as a team.

- Motivated by attending training sessions vs motivated by developing their skills.

- Motivated by achieving a monthly bonus vs motivated by fear of failure.

- Motivated by statistics vs motivated by improvement opportunities.

- Motivated by having the will to win vs motivated by having the will to train to win.

- Motivated by taking credit for wins vs motivated by sharing credit for wins.

- Motivated by blaming others for losses vs motivated by internalising losses.

> Practice does not make perfect; practice makes permanent. Practice perfect

Self-help Motivation

Here's how you can understand, tap into, and use both types of motivation, external and internal, to align with your intentions, keep pushing forward, and overcome the slumps and obstacles that affect your daily sales life.

1. Internal motivation

The key factor driving high achievers towards their purpose is the development of their intrinsic or internal motivation. They don't just intend to do something, they have *intent*.

It's important to understand that a salesperson with a high level of focus and internal motivation can often be misjudged. Their day-to-day interactions are not necessarily understood by colleagues or those who aren't on the same journey.

That's because these highly focused individuals block out unhelpful noise and sometimes appear to be introverted and withdrawn, as opposed to lesser achievers being gregarious and outgoing. A self-motivated person doesn't need external rewards or pats on the back to become a high achiever.

Here are some self-help tips you can use to develop your internal motivation.

- Stay connected to your planned future by regularly setting measurable goals under your intentions. For example, you can aim to pick your children up from school at least once a week. Alternatively, you can plan a monthly meeting with your sales support team to receive feedback and identify improvement areas.

- Pair yourself up with a mentor or trusted advisor, preferably one with the expertise and experience to listen to your questions and share your experiences through personal insights and constructive feedback. An internal mentor can assist you to better engage with the workplace and deal with day-to-day issues and uncertainties. An external mentor is more useful for providing feedback on your career progression, where you are going and how you can get there.

- Study and mirror the sales techniques of successful sellers you have identified from within your company, at sales seminars, or through online resources. Eliminate their unhelpful beliefs and adopt those that align with your values.

- Build an extended support team within your business. Find out what others need from you and how you can serve them. By serving others, you encourage them to serve you in return. An example would be to ensure you ask your logistics team for advice before booking or offering buyers a service they may be stretched to deliver.

- Develop a routine that works for you. Go to the gym at the same time every day. Aim to be effective and efficient, not just efficient. For example, prioritise picking up the phone and communicating in person instead of sending long-winded emails. Build your daily processes around buyers and customers, not internal meetings and writing reports.

- Don't waste work time by indulging in office gossip, internal politics, waiting for emails to respond to, or constantly checking your social media feeds.

2. External motivation

Is there a place for external motivation? The answer is yes. In some circumstances, external motivation can be beneficial. For example, when you are asked to perform tasks that you have no internal desire to accomplish. If the request is accompanied by an external reward like a meal voucher or a bonus, it can become more motivating.

In other instances, when you meet monthly performance standards or receive praise or an unexpected reward, these can serve to increase, not decrease, internal motivation. Employers that provide external motivation through regular training seminars and quality learning opportunities can also increase your job satisfaction and internal motivation.

In general, being reliant on external motivation and rewards is not enough to achieve your sales purpose.

Consistently receiving praise and rewards for tasks that come easily to you or align with your passion for sales can eventually lead to a counterproductive effect, by making them feel like hard work. In many sales-driven organisations, the prevailing belief is to motivate sales teams by offering excessive praise and financial incentives for reaching revenue targets, even if they are relatively modest.

If your motivation becomes solely fixated on meeting these targets and you start considering them as the sole measure of excellence, it can eventually lead to complacency and hinder your career growth.

This mindset may result in a diminished drive to keep learning and an expectation of additional rewards for achieving standards that you previously considered as a baseline or minimum expectation of yourself.

Being reliant on external motivation and
rewards is not enough to achieve your
sales purpose.

Key Takeaways

Achieving a successful sales career is unlikely to happen by
chance unless you possess exceptional talent or are very
lucky. It requires a heightened determination and the
development of a plan that aligns with your purpose, values,
and a clear vision of the lifestyle you aspire to.

While external motivation is valuable for meeting short-
term objectives, your internal drive and motivation are
fuelled by your intent rather than mere intentions. Internal
motivation is not a one-stop shop; it must be cultivated over
time. As your life progresses, your goals, aspirations, and
motivations evolve accordingly.

Chapter Two:
Listening is a Skill

Every salesperson knows that listening is the most important of all sales skills. After all, poor listening skills can result in lost revenue, misunderstandings, errors, and the erosion of trust between buyers and sellers.

While being a good listener may seem easy, the reality is that many sellers struggle to pay attention and genuinely listen to what their buyers are saying.

Please don't interrupt me while I'm
interrupting you

The old saying of "please don't interrupt me while I'm interrupting you" refers to people who try to steal time from those who need more time. It's also the classic stereotype of a salesperson who's more interested in listening to themselves than the voice of their buyers.

The reason listening is such an important sales skill is simple. Those who have mastered it are the most successful. While their competitors are feigning interest, a good listener stands out and positively differentiates themselves simply by being attentive and giving buyers their undivided attention. They not only diagnose and solve the buyer's problem, but also understand their motivation.

Why Salespeople Struggle to Listen

There's a big difference between *hearing* what's being said and *listening* to what's being said. Listening involves understanding the true meaning of what's being said. Here are some of the primary reasons why many salespeople struggle to listen.

- They would rather be talking, as it addresses a need for control and attention, rather than listening to others.

- They have their own agenda and see everything else as small talk until they can direct the conversation to what interests them.

- They want to interject and have stopped listening while they look for a pause or a space so they can join the conversation.

- They are multitasking by web surfing or checking their devices and responding to emails and social media updates while the speaker is talking.

- They have a contrary opinion to the speaker and stop listening until it's their turn to speak. They become preoccupied with proving the speaker wrong.

- They are framing their response instead of listening. This is exacerbated if there's a perception the speaker is being critical or overly negative.

- The speaker is longwinded or boring and uninteresting. The listener starts daydreaming and tunes out until it's their turn to talk.

Test your listening skills by taping a sales call and telling a colleague what you heard. Review the call with the same person and see if what you think you heard is what was actually said. The result might surprise you!

Active Listening and Quality Conversations

Buyers are savvy. They know when their voices aren't being listening to. Active listening is a pattern of listening to and responding to another person in a way that keeps both parties engaged in a positive way. It is an essential sales skill that enables clarity and mutual understanding. It also facilitates quality conversations.

Communication is not a one-way process. It requires, at least, someone to give the message and someone to receive it. The ability to conduct a quality conversation is the foundation of sales success. It requires the salesperson to ask questions and be prepared to listen while also observing non-verbal messages.

You can improve and enhance your on-the-job listening and conversational skills by practicing some straightforward techniques.

- Avoid the temptation to multitask. While on the phone, make a point of turning off your devices or ignoring email, social media, and text messages. It's preferable to find neutral turf by moving away from your desk and these distractions.

- Don't interrupt the speaker. If you're on the phone or a video link, a good technique is to mute your voice when your buyer is talking, then unmute it when it's time for you to speak. This forces you to listen without interjecting.

- If your buyer is overly deliberate or a slow talker, this doesn't mean they need encouragement or reinforcement. Slow your tempo to match theirs rather than try to speed them up.

- As buyers respond to your questions, it's important to give affirmations and feedback to their responses. At regular intervals, reflect and restate their feelings and important information back to them. The buyer can correct any misunderstandings and more importantly, know they are being understood.

- Buyers can become confused or overwhelmed by their feelings or the complexity of the decisions they must make. If they start rambling or get off track, bring them back to a practical level by restating the known facts, not the variables and unknowns.

- You are there to facilitate the conversation. If there are long pauses or gaps while the buyer is thinking, avoid the temptation to interrupt, over talk, and take over by filling the gaps. Silences are often a salesperson's best friend.

- Whatever you do, keep things conversational and don't machine gun your questions or stack them one after the other. A quality conversation is only achieved if there is a genuine flow, rapport, and empathy during the questioning process.

- Some buyers are very guarded and economical with their words. Draw them out with a combination of open and closed questions. Start with easy questions and revert to more probing ones once they are more relaxed.

Nonverbal Communication

Nonverbal communication can be either conscious or subconscious. Any time you conduct a face-to-face buyer meeting (irrespective of location), there are some important nonverbal cues and messages you should be aware of. Some are the buyers, and some are your own. Here are some examples.

- First impressions count. Think carefully about your appearance and if it's appropriate for the brand you represent. While it's important to celebrate diversity, you should still consider what nonverbal messages you are sending and if that will affect your ability to connect with the buyer. A warm smile, of course, costs nothing.

- How you arrange personal space for a sit-down meeting is very important. The distance between you has an influence on the signals sent and received. Avoid being in the buyer's intimate or personal space by keeping a reasonable distance (1.5–3 m) apart. This is called the social consultative zone. Attempt to sit together, but at right angles. This creates a semi-relaxed but professional atmosphere. By its very nature, direct, face-to-face contact can be viewed as confrontational and overly formal.

- Turn your phone off, sit upright, and give the buyer your full attention. Make eye contact and signal encouragement when they speak. This conveys that you are listening and understand what's being said. Continuous eye contact may, however, be perceived as staring or intimidating. Things like pen clicking, frowning, checking your phone, waving hands around, fidgeting, and moving around should be avoided.

- Observe the buyer's nonverbal behaviour. Their voice could be saying one thing while their body language says something else. If there's a discrepancy, what they're saying nonverbally is likely closer to their real feelings. For example: they may be speaking calmly yet exhibit signs of tension through clenched fists or a tight jawline.

- Take into account that nonverbal communication can be strongly influenced by cultural context. As an example, in some cultures, making direct eye contact is considered rude and disrespectful. In others, it is considered a sign of trust and respect.

Key Takeaways

Irrespective of your experience level, mastering the art of active listening and developing your ability to engage in quality conversations are essential to a successful sales career. These skills serve as powerful differentiators that will set you apart from your competitors and their approaches. When you show genuine interest and give buyers your undivided attention, you not only identify their challenges but also understand their motivations, resulting in more successful sales outcomes.

Chapter Three:
Develop Your Sales EQ

If you want to achieve consistent sales success, it's essential to develop your Sales EQ (emotional quotient) skills. Sales EQ is best described as the ability to understand, manage, and leverage your emotions and those of others in order to build relationships and drive sales. It involves using empathy, self-awareness, social skills, motivation, and self-regulation to connect with your buyers.

In today's world, your buyers have an abundance of options, including digital solutions where technology takes over and tells them what to do. The value of developing your Sales EQ lies in its capacity to satisfy a universal desire for genuine and authentic human interaction. When you can comprehend and relate to the emotional needs of your buyers, it becomes possible to connect in a way that resonates and makes them feel understood and appreciated. This quality sets you apart from the competition and helps buyers understand why selecting you is the best option.

So how do you get started with Sales EQ? Simply put, integrating EQ into your sales approach is no different from how you apply it to your everyday life. When you focus on enhancing your EQ, the benefits will be obvious not only in sales, but also in personal relationships. It all starts with honing your ability to perceive and interpret emotions in yourself and others, then using this awareness to manage behaviours, build those relationships, and generate more sales.

Essential Sales Traits

Most of us know a sales professional who has achieved great success by moving through multiple career stages and enjoying the rewards. In most instances, you will find they have progressively developed and refined their Sales EQ to an extremely high level. Here are some of the traits of a salesperson with exceptional Sales EQ.

- They follow a prescribed process and stay in that process. This works from the buyer's doorstep back to their own, not vice versa.

- They listen to understand, not to respond. They comprehend the buyer's emotions and can successfully label and articulate these emotions back to them. Their genuineness impresses.

- They are not afraid to challenge a buyer's assumptions and assist them in uncovering their real needs. As they work through the sales process, they build a clear picture of these needs and move beyond complexity to develop solutions that work.

- They know when to accelerate and close the sale. They are outcome-focussed, but for the buyer first. They don't present their solution and walk away. If there are delays or obstacles, they adjust quickly and stay in the process until the buyer has made a firm commitment.

Getting Started – The Self-Assessment

The first step of your Sales EQ journey is to conduct a thorough self-assessment and gain insight into your strengths and weaknesses. It's crucial to be honest with yourself during this process; hence the need for a specific checklist to work through each of these Sales EQ pillars.

1. Self-Awareness – Knowing yourself and your impact on others.

    In your day-to-day sales activities, do your body language and speech reflect the values and culture of the brand you represent? Do you know your own personal brand and how you impact others? Do you lack genuineness when you meet a buyer?

2. Self-management and Regulation – Redirecting disruptive emotions.

    Do you realise you are at war and must capture buyers from competitors – and are you giving your best effort every day? Do you follow a structured process and ignore the temptation to take shortcuts? Do you keep a cool head when under pressure from buyers or unexpected changes?

3. Social Skills – Managing relationships.

    Do you manage your biases and build rapport in a positive way? Do you genuinely attempt to understand each buyer's motivations and needs before moving them in the desired direction? Alternatively, do you adopt a practical, simplistic, and tactical approach? Do you often end up in the bargain basement? Do you anticipate questions and roadblocks by preparing in advance to counter them?

4. Empathy – Considering the feelings of others.

   Are you genuinely capable of listening attentively and putting yourself in the buyer's shoes? Alternatively, do you listen to respond, not to understand? Are you communicating with your buyer's needs in mind or is it all about what you are trying to achieve? Do you label a buyer's feelings back to them to confirm you have been listening and genuinely understand their circumstances?

5. Motivation – Being driven to achieve.

   Is sales just a job or is it your profession? Are you a learner who understands that a sales career is a journey, not a destination? Alternatively, are you a sales zombie, intent on survival and acting on autopilot? Do you lack confidence and suffer from imposter syndrome? Or are you overconfident and take credit for all successes while externalising failures? Have you become disengaged and ineffective by using technology to avoid quality human interaction with your buyers?

Your Sales EQ Journey

Although your employer may or may not provide a sales learning environment, the reality is that each individual must make a commitment to their own personal development and growth. Once you've conducted a thorough self-assessment, you can begin your journey towards improved Sales EQ. It's important to remember that developing and fine-tuning these skills is a continuous process that will extend over your full working life. Like any journey, there must be a starting point.

Here are some suggestions for getting things underway.

Find your personal brand

Having self-awareness gives us the ability to understand ourselves and reestablish our real identities through transparency and genuineness. If you've taken the time to perform an honest self-appraisal, you will understand if you lack authenticity and are wearing an artificial sales mask.

> "It occurred to me that I was not the person I thought I was, but rather the person the majority of other people thought I was."
>
> ~ David Bowie on his Ziggy Stardust

David Bowie, a legendary English musician, invented a fictional character and stage persona named Ziggy Stardust. Ziggy, who had a pale and androgynous appearance, was an alien-like figure donning glamorous attire and sporting a vibrant, red mullet. From 1971 to 1973, Bowie produced various Ziggy Stardust albums and performed alongside his supporting band, The Spiders from Mars. His popularity skyrocketed, and he is widely regarded as the pioneer of glam rock.

During a concert in July 1973, David Bowie announced the death of Ziggy Stardust. This would be Ziggy's last performance. He then relocated to the United States and transformed himself into a soul and funk artist.

Bowie's rationale for retiring the character of Ziggy Stardust was that he sensed he was losing touch with his own identity and perspective.

Similar to how Bowie shed his persona of Ziggy Stardust, a self-aware salesperson can make comparable adjustments to change how they are perceived by others.

Find your personal blind spots

Our blind spots are hidden areas in our character and behaviour that others use to evaluate, judge, and label us, whether consciously or unconsciously, often as a first impression. They play a significant role in shaping our personal brand and how we are perceived by others.

Blind spots can be either positive or negative, being obvious to others but not to ourselves. The only way to understand them is by soliciting open and honest feedback from others.

Here's a real-life example of how my own blind spot was negatively impacting both my ability to lead others and perform to my potential.

Early in my career as the country manager of a global corporation, I prided myself on leading some significant initiatives around workplace culture, leadership, people, and performance. One of our initiatives was an anonymous 360-degree feedback review.

The first time we did this, I had high expectations. However, when the results came in, there were some scathing criticisms about my performance. The consensus was that it is challenging to respect and work for someone who swears all the time, with one respondent even suggesting that I be fired on those grounds.

The 360-degree feedback I received presented an opportunity to enhance my emotional quotient (EQ) and become more effective in my role. My good work was ineffective because I was unaware of the negative impact my language had on the feelings of others. In essence, 95 percent of my good work was being undone by a 5-percent flaw in my day-to-day interactions.

The solution was to modify my language and stop swearing. This was easier said than done. To achieve the right outcome, I asked several senior executives to fine me every time I uttered a profanity in a meeting or presentation.

Find your sales blind spots

For a salesperson to understand the blind spots that affect their performance, they must first have a genuine desire to solicit and act upon constructive feedback from others. The 360-degree feedback is an obvious internal method, but that's not generally job-specific. You need to know what *buyers* are thinking.

One effective way to receive genuine feedback is to have a sales colleague accompany you on sales calls or listen to your own recorded calls.

> Be willing to take honest feedback, even if it may be critical or uncomfortable.

Based on my experience, it's surprising how many opportunities to close a sale are offered by buyers but are overlooked by the salesperson. This is usually due to their preoccupation with scripted questions or being fixated with following the sales process and forgetting to listen.

Conversely, some salespeople are convinced they have closed a sale based upon a vague discussion where no offer was made or accepted. By having a third party listen to your sales conversations and provide honest feedback, you will quickly identify blind spots and areas where you can fine-tune your approach.

It's important to keep an open mind and be willing to take honest feedback, even if it may be critical or uncomfortable.

The role-playing of buyer meetings as a training exercise, including phone and video calls, can be very effective, especially when followed by an open and transparent feedback session. It's a great way to build confidence and team cohesion, particularly when it becomes a regular part of the sales culture within your organisation. By practicing role-playing, you can be exposed to a wide range of situations and see how different sales approaches can yield different outcomes.

Unfortunately, some companies only use role-playing exercises during their annual sales conference, which can create added pressure and stress rather than becoming a learning opportunity. If you encourage your sales team to incorporate regular role-playing exercises into weekly routines, you can minimize anxiety and optimise the benefits of the exercise.

Compare yourself to competitors

Many companies use mystery shoppers to function as undercover buyers. These are field-based researchers employed by consulting companies. Mystery shoppers are hired to engage with businesses to specifically assess their sales approach and performance. They are usually provided with specific guidelines and evaluation metrics by the client organisation.

For individual salespeople, mystery shopper reports are an invaluable tool for evaluating the effectiveness of their sales approach and performance. They can identify improvement areas, training opportunities, and give direct apples-to-apples comparisons with competitors.

Given that one of your primary objectives is to capture revenue from competitors, the use of mystery shoppers will provide you with an unbiased view of what's working, where your blind spots are, and what needs urgent attention.

Key Takeaways

Sales EQ is all about understanding, managing, and leveraging emotions, to build relationships and drive sales. It's no surprise that the majority of successful sales professionals have developed and refined their Sales EQ to an extremely high level. If you invest time into identifying and addressing your blind spots, while incorporating EQ into your daily sales approach, you will satisfy your buyers needs for genuine and authentic human interaction. Not only will this set you apart from your competitors, it will also result in more sales.

Chapter Four:
Winning Tips for Sales Professionals

Achieving success in sales requires much more than just being involved – it requires a certain DNA that is shared by all successful sales professionals. These individuals are learners and are fully invested in their own growth and development.

It's not just about leveraging strengths, but also putting time and effort into understanding and enhancing their improvement areas. They take what they learn and apply it in the real world, fine-tuning their techniques along the way.

Here are five winning tips to help you consistently achieve sales success.

1. Play a TEAM game

Salespeople in many companies are often subjected to stigmas, ranging from being perceived as lazy and unmotivated to being seen as pushy, arrogant, and dishonest. Unless changed, these perceptions can limit effectiveness and adversely affect their performance.

Sales is a collaborative effort, and successful salespeople do not work alone or fly solo. They represent the tip of a vast spearhead, with the collective mindset, knowledge, and resources of their entire organisation supporting them.

This does not happen automatically. Professional salespeople excel at managing their one-person business within the company. If you're unhappy with the sales support and culture provided by your extended team, don't expect it to change unless you take the initiative to lead the change. As the tip of the spear, you can adopt an internal leadership role and inspire others to support you by pushing in the same direction.

To initiate and lead a positive change in the sales environment, your first step is to solicit candid feedback on how others perceive you. Developing your self-awareness and comprehending how you're viewed by your colleagues and superiors is critical to embarking on a leadership journey.

For instance, do you offer buyers incentives or unrealistic timelines without consulting management and your customer service teams? Are you self-absorbed and uninterested in the abilities and contributions of your colleagues? Do you ever ask them how you can improve *their* work lives?

Through self-assessment and using internal feedback to make positive changes, you can effectively assume responsibility for your personal brand. This approach enables you to quickly dispel negative stereotypes, improve your sales outcomes, and establish a reputation as a valuable contributor to your company's success.

2. Prioritise Effectiveness over Efficiency

In today's world, efficiency experts and systems are driving our day-to-day work lives, to the detriment of actual human contact. It has become a social norm and expectation that we communicate frequently and respond to messages in real time, regardless of whether it's for work or personal purposes. Being busy, for many, is sitting at our desks, waiting for new messages to respond to. Even the customer relationship management (CRM) systems we use are focused on time-consuming data inputs.

For a salesperson, effective time management can be the difference between success and failure. With the constant distractions of social media, technology, and demanding daily routines, even top performers can lose focus. While lengthy email communication, immediate message responses, and endless meetings may seem efficient, they do not necessarily lead to more sales. Constantly checking phone messages and social media accounts are timewasters that add little to our professional lives.

If you want to be one of the best, you need to prioritise being both effective *and* efficient over just being efficient, even if it means going against the flow and established norms. The less time you spend on distractions and meaningless tasks, the more one-on-one time you'll have to cultivate relationships with buyers, which will then lead to the closing of more deals.

3. Open a Trust Account and Make a Deposit

The ability to build strong relationships is the foundation of a successful sales career. That's why sales professionals stick to a structured sales process. The combination of a structured sales process, a buyer-led approach, and progressive relationship-building techniques serves to improve buyer engagement, differentiate sellers from their competitors, and ultimately lead to consistent sales success.

A great way for you to build relationships with buyers is to open a trust account and then make a deposit. This can be as simple as meeting a buyer and committing to follow up with additional research or information they will find useful. This technique demonstrates that you are invested in their success and willing to go above and beyond to help them achieve their goals.

It can also be a great opportunity to introduce other team members who can provide specialised insights or expertise, further demonstrating your commitment to the buyer's success. It's important to note that all information should be offered unconditionally; the objective is to build the relationship, not to leverage the buyer or appear disingenuous.

To elevate your sales strategy, consider implementing an unannounced surprise callback. Here's how it works. During your Q&A or discovery process, you may have uncovered needs that your buyer is unaware of. If you make a surprise callback to share this information and discuss potential solutions, the buyer will feel appreciated and valued.

This advanced relationship-building technique helps establish a strong connection with buyers and positions you as a valuable partner in their decision-making journey. In some cases, your insights may challenge their perspective, as they were in control and following their own process until you introduced new information from left field.

This strategy is most effective when introduced later in the sales process, as it limits the buyer's opportunity to use your insights to educate your competitors. By postponing the presentation of critical new information and leveraging the element of surprise, you can take control of the buyer's decision-making process and accelerate the sales cycle.

4. Seek First to Understand

A solution-driven sales approach starts with the buyer's end game in mind. The objective is to first understand, and then to be understood. That means asking a lot of questions and *listening to learn*, rather than respond.

With this in mind, one of a good salesperson's first questions should relate to what the buyer is hoping to achieve, and what a successful outcome will mean to them. During the discovery process, be prepared to challenge the buyer's perceptions and dig bone-deep to understand any specific needs or pain points they may be unaware of.

Following are some examples of how you can customize your approach by filling in the gaps from the buyer's end game back to the present.

- Introduce them to an in-house expert to provide technical advice and guidance on any specific issues or concerns. By doing so, you can take the buyer beyond just making a decision and help them visualise a positive outcome. This can empower the buyer to effectively close their own sale and sell themselves on your offering.

- Prior to finalising your sales proposals, consider consulting with your peer group, service delivery team, or manager to discuss and fine-tune your proposed strategy. It's important to be open to critique and alternative ideas and solutions. Unfortunately, many salespeople only seek this type of feedback when they are facing the possibility of losing a booking, rather than proactively planning how to win one.

- Once you've established the basis of your proposal, you can firm things up by collaborating with internal team(s) to plan the perfect outcome for your buyer. This can involve pre-booking or pencilling in necessary resources in advance, with a designated sunset clause or time limit for holding the booking. By doing so, you can highlight to the buyer the importance of acting quickly to secure their desired outcome.

- Prepare a clear, step-by-step timeline from the buyer's vision of the future and then map it back to the present. It can be surprising how often timing becomes a key factor in the purchase. The buyer will often have less time than originally thought, which can serve to accelerate the offer-and-acceptance process – and your chances of winning the business.

5. Get Outside Your Comfort Zone

In all aspects of life, the real magic happens when we step outside our comfort zones. Our comfort zones provide a sense of safety but are also self-limiting and inhibit us from taking risks and progressing. Even with regular training and exposure to new concepts, we tend to revert straight back to our old habits, much like a rubber band that is stretched but snaps back to its original shape. This is our comfort zone.

Some of the common reasons for sellers losing their stretch are as follows.

- The desire to be liked often impedes their ability to push back and challenge their buyer's ideas and perceptions. They tend to adopt the buyer's beliefs rather than discovering underlying needs and pain points to find the best solution. The issue with this approach is that the buyer remains in control. When the buyer sees no differences, they will typically choose the individual they like the most and request that they match the lowest price.

- They are highly opinionated and may unconsciously or consciously stereotype their buyers based on factors such as ethnicity, gender, or social status. For example, a commonly held assumption is that men are the ultimate decision-makers. As a result, some salespeople may not genuinely listen to women because they assume that a male associate or partner will ultimately make the purchasing decision.

- Certain salespeople may excel at various stages of the sales process, but feel extremely uncomfortable discussing money, handling objections, and asking for business. When it comes time to close the deal, they may shy away and hide behind emails, then make excuses for not following up in person. This opens the door for competitors to swoop in and secure the sale. After putting in a significant effort, these salespeople will retreat and leave the outcome to chance when it's time to take things to the next level.

> Wear a rubber band: The magic happens outside your comfort zone, not within it.

Key Takeaways

If you find yourself feeling unmotivated, taking shortcuts, or lacking confidence, a good technique is to wear a rubber band on your wrist. At regular intervals during the day, stretch the rubber band and snap it back into place. The sudden jolt serves as a reminder to move back outside your comfort zone to where the magic happens.

Chapter Five:
Your Ego Is Not Your Amigo

When we talk about ego, we are referring to our sense of self and how we perceive our identity. In simple terms, our egos are the parts of us that are in contact with the real world. They enjoy control and thrive on approval, which can also obscure how others perceive and view us. This isn't news, as most of us are critical of egos and believe that many societies and institutions are both ruled and ruined by egotistical behaviour.

Types of Ego

Whatever type of ego you have, the reality is that it got you to the position you're in right now. The question to ask yourself is, are you satisfied with where you are, and is that where you want to be? If the answer is yes, there's no need to read any further.

Is your ego unhealthy or healthy? Here are some of the characteristics of each.

Unhealthy Egos

Salespeople are often stereotyped, the most common one being the belief that they have exaggerated egos. An egotistical salesperson is one who presents an inflated sense of their own importance, believing they are more intelligent, cleverer, and more knowledgeable than others. If someone is labelled as egocentric, it is because they are seen as being self-centred, lacking empathy, and only interested in themselves. Both of these types of ego can be considered unhealthy and career-limiting.

There are plenty of unhealthy egos working in sales roles. Even the poorest performers can easily overestimate their abilities, believing that despite all evidence to the contrary, they are better than everyone else.

At the other end of the spectrum are those who create an alter ego, in fear of being exposed as a fraud. They are effectively wearing the mask of an egotist as a form of self-medication to disguise and protect their feelings of self-doubt. This condition is often referred to as the imposter syndrome.

Healthy Egos

Successful salespeople understand there's a distinction between an unhealthy and a healthy ego. There's no reason why you shouldn't love yourself or be proud of your achievements if these traits are mixed with humility, authenticity, diplomacy, and an understanding of your impact on others.

Albert Einstein EGO = 1/Knowledge

"The more knowledge you have, the lesser the ego you would have."

Sales professionals with a healthy ego often possess strong emotional intelligence, problem-solving skills, and great confidence in their ability to tackle challenges. For some, it may mean maintaining a low-key demeanour because they are so confident in their skills and abilities, there's no need to prove themselves.

Your Ego Is Not Your Amigo

The phrase *your ego is not your amigo* reminds us there is no room for unhealthy egos in a successful sales career. That's because egotists are focused on themselves, not the buyer and their needs. They restrict themselves from seeing another's heart or considering their point of view.

We all know people with oversized egos. They are the individuals we tend to view negatively and avoid, both in business and in life. Our buyers are no different. That's why it's rare for an egotist to enjoy sales success – beyond their own feelings of self-importance and rhetoric.

One of the characteristics of an unhealthy ego is the tendency of its owner to be totally oblivious to their shortcomings. Friends and family may consider their self-serving behaviour as a loveable personality trait. They may even openly joke about it. However, this level of acceptance doesn't carry over to our professional lives. That's why many salespeople struggle to acknowledge or accept the need for change, even when they're challenged or given constructive feedback from a buyer, colleague, or their manager.

How to Win by Keeping Your Ego in Check

Not all salespeople have unhealthy egos. The ones who don't are generally the high achievers who enjoy the lifestyle, job satisfaction, and financial rewards that come with a successful career in sales. Their focus is on serving others.

Here are some strategies for getting out of your own way and keeping your ego checked and under control.

1. Adopt humility as a core value.

Being humble isn't about thinking less of yourself, it's about thinking of yourself less. You have a quiet confidence and an appreciation of your own abilities; you don't go around looking for applause and the approval of others. You have a willingness to view yourself accurately while also appreciating the strengths of others and showing gratitude for their contributions. Humility is directly related to your willingness and ability to take feedback. Humble people openly acknowledge mistakes and use them as learning experiences.

When you choose to adopt a humble approach, you walk in a friendlier world. It enables you to foster positive relationships with everyone, not just your buyers. Take every opportunity to interact with and learn from your internal service teams and colleagues. If you take the time to discuss how you can support each other both before and after you've made a sale, they will quickly become your allies. If their advice helps you find the solution to a buyer's problem (and win the sale), go back with a thank-you and acknowledgement of their contribution.

"For the strength of the pack is the wolf,
and the strength of the wolf is the pack."

~Rudyard Kipling,
The Second Jungle Book, 1895

What this quote means is that the strength of your whole team is more important than your strength as an individual. If you and your colleagues work together and support each other, your sales outcomes and job satisfaction will far surpass what you could achieve individually.

2. Stay in your sales process.

The best sales processes promote asking questions and listening to your buyers in front of showcasing your knowledge, suggesting relevant options/solutions, and trying to close the deal.

While the tempo of your process might vary, it's important to stick to that process and tick all the boxes. That means listening to and understanding the needs and emotions of your buyers before identifying the right solution and presenting it to them.

If you meet a personality, you vibe with, it doesn't automatically mean they will buy from you. Alternatively, if you run into an unpleasant or difficult personality, it also doesn't mean you won't make the sale. You will enjoy consistent success if you stick to the process.

3. Mirror the A-Sellers

Mirroring is a term that refers to the copying of sales-specific strategies, tactics, and behaviours from others. A-Sellers are the ones who consistently achieve their sales goals and demonstrate the habits and behaviours you admire and aspire to.

The purpose of mirroring the A-Sellers is to improve your sales knowledge and unlock your potential through learning from the best. You may just be interested in a specific questioning technique or how they manage and utilize their office time. A-Sellers are generally very approachable if you come from a genuine place. They got to be top performers through talent and hard work, not trying to outgun their colleagues.

Outside of your direct team, there's a multitude of opportunities to mirror A-Sellers. Many of the world's best salespeople have built or contributed to digital eLearning platforms, host regular podcasts, and exchange ideas with other sellers in interactive global forums. Then there's the opportunity to learn in person, by attending sales seminars and conferences, most of which are hosted by A-Sellers. These events can also be great motivators.

4. Don't compete with your buyer's ego.

Everything that applies to your ego also applies to buyer's. As you meet them, you will quickly identify the ones with the big egos. They know everything, think they're better than you, want to beat down your price, or want to cut to the chase. Some will delight in treating you and colleagues as underlings. They will also be comparing you and your services with competitors, and probably let you know about it.

No matter how you feel, resist the temptation to beat an egotist at their own game. Remember, a bad ending generally follows a bad beginning. Even if they buddy up to you, don't get into a game of cat and mouse. The way to secure their business is to stay in your sales process, always be positive, and win them over with your professionalism and genuine interest in their needs.

Don't skip the questions just because they're trying to dominate you. Because they think they know everything, you will uncover plenty of issues and needs they never knew they had. Early in your process, resist the temptation to discuss these; that can come later. If you do, they will take credit for your insights and use this information to brief your competitors. The more you teach them, the more likely you are to lose the sale.

When it's time to challenge their thinking and deliver new information, focus on how your solution will make them feel, in addition to the technical and practical aspects. The emotional benefits are harder for them to quantify, especially if there are others involved (e.g., their partner or family members).

Up to this point, they have been in total control and primarily concerned with getting a good deal. It's unlikely they've even considered the bigger picture, including the emotional and financial consequences of making the wrong decision.

If your egotistical buyer considers themselves a supreme negotiator, avoid the temptation to offer an upfront discount. Ask for the full price or rack rate so they know you place a high value on your services/products. If and when you allow them to negotiate a discount, they will be drawn into comparing the difference between the reduced price and your rack rate, not your competitors' price.

Remember, if you find a buyer overbearing or distasteful, you won't be alone. Your competitors will feel the same. In these situations, your chances of winning can be higher than if you're dealing with a people pleaser, simply by staying on task and lasting the distance.

5. Avoid being defensive.

One of the best ways to keep your ego in check is to avoid being defensive. This is not as easy as it sounds. For example, you might be following up a proposal or presenting your solution and are met with a negative response or complete rejection.

Your immediate reaction will probably be an overwhelming urge to defend yourself and convince the buyer they're wrong. This is the worst thing you can do. You have now made it about yourself, not your proposal.

If a buyer doesn't see the value in what you're offering, it's unlikely they will change their mind at that moment. If you push back hard, they may even dig their toes in and turn a maybe or I'll consider it into an outright rejection.

The better reaction would be to express your disappointment and ask for feedback on where things went wrong. You may have missed something, or your proposal lacked clarity and didn't resonate. They may not see any difference between the value you are offering compared to others, so price became an issue. If you're being genuine, most buyers will willingly tell you.

Once they've clarified their concerns, ask for an opportunity to review your bid based upon their feedback. Make an appointment to get back to them with a revised proposal, preferably within a short timeframe. This way, they won't feel you're wasting their time.

If you do this correctly, you have turned things around and positioned yourself to win their business. You will be top of mind, and your second effort will be a customised solution based upon their direct feedback.

Key Takeaways

An unhealthy ego can prove highly detrimental to a successful sales career. Not only does it hinder a salesperson's ability to collaborate and foster internal teamwork, but it also prioritises their emotional needs over those of the buyer. There's an old saying of unknown origin: "In the battle of the giant egos, the loser always wins." This adage teaches us that even if the seller manages to impose their will or outwit a similarly egotistical buyer, they are highly likely to lose the sale. It's far better to lose this battle and secure the order than the other way around.

Sales success requires humility, empathy, and a willingness to listen, learn, and adapt. This can only be achieved by cultivating a healthy ego that fosters a genuine buyer-centric mindset. Sales is a team game, and the priority of the team is to deliver solutions that resonate and consistently turn potential buyers into paying customers.

PART 2

SALES

INSIGHTS

Stuff You Need to Know

No matter what industry sector you are in or what you are selling, the job description of all salespeople ultimately comes down to the same thing. Your job is to capture value from your competitors by turning buyers into customers.

The saying that knowledge is power is especially true in today's fast-paced and highly competitive sales landscape.

If you are living in the past, chances are that you are practicing the art of ABC (Always Be Closing). Don't worry, there's still time to change. If you don't, the risk of early retirement to the job loss cemetery is beckoning.

This section offers valuable insight into the daily challenges encountered by salespeople.

Read on and be ready to elevate your understanding of the FUNdamentals of selling and learn some important stuff that you really need to know. For example, did you know you can double your revenue by just making a few tweaks to your current process?

Chapter One:
Buyers Are in Control

Without a doubt, in today's era, the power dynamic has shifted away from sellers and their employers towards the buyers. Buyers are in control.

With access to vast amounts of information, buyers can now meticulously research and choose with whom they do business. Gone are the days when advertising holds sway over them. They have access to an oversupply of consumer feedback scores and price information from multiple suppliers for comparable products. In fact, many business leaders maintain that staying relevant and in touch with consumer purchasing habits is their greatest challenge.

Another factor influencing the shift of power from sellers to buyers is that in every sector, there is more competition. For a relatively low cost, new entrants or under-resourced businesses can now quickly position themselves as credible alternatives to the established market leaders and heritage brands.

All they need is a pay-per-click advertising campaign, an attractive website, and social media presence. Their messaging can even be copied and pasted from a market leader's digital platforms. Many businesses, both new and established, are adopting innovative technologies to streamline their operations, enabling 24/7 functioning from anywhere.

With the majority of buyers having easy access to digital resources, there are also plenty of opportunities for sellers to meet their needs with little or no human interaction at all. If there's little difference between the available alternatives, these buyers will base their purchasing decisions on who provides the most seamless end-to-end digital experience. In general, this approach is popular when the problem and solution are already known, and the focus is on a particular product or products.

Buyers Are Not Customers

In sales you deal with buyers, not customers. This distinction can be confusing, and easily leads to complacency and lost opportunities.

There is a significant difference between a buyer and a customer. A buyer is a person who is considering making a purchase of goods or services, whereas a customer is someone who has already made the purchase and is now the end user.

Think about it. How many times have you or your colleagues lost or had to recover a sale after assuming a potential buyer had already become a customer?

Just because someone gives you positive feedback or agrees to a deal verbally, it doesn't mean they will buy from you. This is particularly important when dealing with buyers who are people pleasers and friendly towards everyone – including your competitors.

> A buyer will only become a customer when
> they have either signed an agreement, paid
> a deposit, or paid in full.

What Buyers Want

Luckily, even in today's crowded business environment, there are still ways to achieve an advantage that can't easily be replicated or cut and pasted. What many of your competitors don't understand is that how you make buyers *feel* can be as important as what you are actually selling. The key is to align your sales process to the buyer's purchasing journey. In essence, how you sell must be buyer-centric, not company-centric.

When making a purchase – and irrespective of who they're dealing with – buyers will commonly take into account several or all of these key factors.

- They want a service partner who will be there when they need them. That means treating them as a priority and responding accordingly.

- They want a service partner who takes the time to listen to, understand, and meet their unique needs.

- They want a service partner who reflects their values and demonstrates a commitment to doing the right thing.

- They want a service partner who's easy to work with; this means in their day-to-day interactions as well as their business practices.

- They want a service partner who makes them feel good and amplifies who they are through positive feedback and recognition.

- They want a service partner who delivers the best value, not necessarily the cheapest. If they pay a little more, they want to feel it's still the best deal.

The Buyer's Purchasing Journey

Typically, buyers don't get out of bed and decide to make a significant purchase on a whim. They undertake a purchasing journey which involves a series of steps and activities to obtain something they need or desire. In all reality, it could just as easily be called their purchasing process.

Look no further than the online dating phenomenon to understand how a typical buyer's purchasing journey evolves. This is important because your sales process needs to be aligned to this journey.

We all know that online dating is one of the most popular, convenient, and flexible ways of meeting prospective partners. Depending on their needs and circumstances, online daters could be looking for anything from a casual friendship through to a life partner. They can move at a snail's pace or with great urgency.

For those seeking tangible outcomes, the steps on their online dating journey are very similar to those they take when they are making a purchasing decision.

Stages	Online Dating Journey	Buyer's Purchasing Journey
Research	• Identify and focus on personal needs and potential solutions. • Research through word of mouth, web, social media. • Join the dating site(s) that meets those needs.	• Identify and focus on specific needs and potential solutions. • Research through word of mouth, web, social media. • Identify a selection of sellers who may meet their needs.
Evaluation	• Sort through thumbnails and profiles, exchange messages and eliminate unsuitable prospects. • Meet a selection in person, based upon initial attraction. • Stay open to alternatives or new options.	• Initiate first contact with selected sellers. • Meet in person, by video, or phone. • Eliminate unsuitable prospects. • Stay open to alternatives or new options.
Comfort	• Through dating and further meetings, identify a shortlist of preferred candidates. • Evaluate levels of attraction, compatibility, trust, and ability to meet future needs. • Stop looking in earnest (but may keep profile open).	• Identify a shortlist of preferred seller(s) by evaluating their products/services. • Consider synergies, levels of trust, ability to deliver a solution, and competitiveness. • Stay open to alternatives or late entrants.

Selection	• Choose the partner who can best meet their criteria and needs. • Announce engagement and start planning a future life together. • Take down online profiles and stop looking for alternatives. • Set a timeline for a wedding date.	• Choose and notify the seller who can deliver the best overall solution. • Stop looking for alternatives. • Plan the next step; start firming up details and timelines for becoming a customer.
The Danger Zone	*It's not a done deal yet! An extended timeline between the engagement and wedding increases the likelihood of unforeseen circumstances, unplanned events, or attractive new candidates disrupting the wedding plans.*	*It's still not a done deal! At this point, sellers must take over and formalise the buyer's commitment as quickly as possible. The longer this takes, the more chance of plans changing or a competitor following up with a new bid.*
Commitment: Putting a ring on the finger.	The journey's end. It's the wedding day. Time to walk up the aisle, put a ring on the finger, and sign the marriage contract.	The journey's end. The purchase order or contract is signed, the deposit banked, the buyer is now a customer

Aligning With the Buyer's Purchasing Journey

In the initial stages of the buyer relationship, your focus is on positioning yourself to make the sale. As they progress through the research, evaluation, and comfort stages of their purchasing journey, you can concentrate on asking questions to uncover their known and unknown needs. During this time frame, you can build trust by introducing thoughtful and relevant observations and insights.

Keep in mind that buyers may not see many differences between you and your competitors, so the features and benefits you have on offer may not be enough to differentiate you from other sellers.

The Buyer Selects You

When it's time for your buyer to select their preferred candidate, they are looking for differences and the wow factor. There's no future in being the same as everyone else. Your secret sauce during their purchasing journey is to have taken every opportunity to differentiate yourself and what you have to offer.

Luckily, this is not as difficult as it sounds. If you stay on the journey, many of your competitors will eliminate themselves.

Here's how you can build upon the essential (and practical) features and benefits of your proposal by introducing positive surprises that will clearly differentiate and elevate you above your competitors.

Features/Benefits What you have, how it benefits	Who	Differentiation and Wow Factor Positive surprises, how they feel	Who
Infrastructure and capability	All	*Show appreciation and empathy.* *Listen, acknowledge, and validate.*	You
Nice, helpful people	All	*Insight into what they want.* *How you can make their life better.*	You
Experience and Knowledge	All	*Identify their hidden needs.* *Give them context and perspective.*	You
Timing and Availability	All	*Focus on clarity, not complexity.* *How your solution makes them feel.*	You
Having a story to tell	All	*A customised solution.* *The perfect outcome, just for them.*	You
Competitive Price and Value	All	*Assistance with their decision.* *Let's proceed and make it happen.*	You

Putting a Ring on the Buyer's Finger

Once you've successfully navigated the selection process of the buyer's purchasing journey, you have been chosen as the 'one' and are effectively engaged to be married.

Many salespeople make the mistake of thinking their buyer has now become a customer. They lose focus and start moving on to the next one. In reality, there's still important work to be done. That's because it's now time to accelerate and get them up the aisle with a ring on their finger as quickly as possible.

The reason for urgency is a simple one. You are now residing in the danger zone, between verbal or informal acceptance and getting the buyer's full commitment. The longer the time gap between these two events, the more susceptible you are to the law of diminishing intent. This law says that the longer the delay in accomplishing something, the less likely you are to get it done.

There's still a lot that can go wrong, including the buyer having a change of plans – or a change of heart. Just like in the dating world, there may be individuals who have agreed to your proposal of engagement but are still receptive to potential advances from previous suitors or new and exciting contenders that appear unexpectedly.

Key Takeaways

There's no doubting that today's buyers really are in charge. They have access to more options, more information, and operate in a fast-paced digital world.

Initially, they may see less difference between you and your competitors than you do. This is why effective salespeople recognize that traditional methods such as Always Be Closing (ABC) are outdated.

Today's sales processes must be tailored to support buyers' thinking and purchasing behaviour. This entails dedicating more time to positioning, to clearly differentiate yourself from the competition. However, once you are positioned as their primary choice, yet not the sole option, it's imperative you accelerate the process and get a ring on their finger as quickly as possible.

Chapter Two:
Sales = Event Management

Irrespective of what you're selling, if you're in sales, you are part of an event management business. By way of definition, an event is anything of importance that happens. Event management literally means the process of successfully planning and delivering something of importance.

To begin with, it's important to recognize that the anticipation of buyer success can only be staged or set up, as concrete outcomes don't materialise until you've made the sale. Your sales challenge is to stage events that motivate potential buyers to consistently select your product or service.

While you should avoid setting unrealistic expectations or making unfulfillable commitments, the goal is to generate a sense of excitement and the expectation of a positive end-user experience. Because events are experiential in nature, these expectations should resonate on both emotional and practical levels.

Have a Servant Culture

> A servant culture breaks down internal silos.

As a salesperson, it's essential you have confidence in the events you plan, stage, and execute with your colleagues. Your internal stakeholders and colleagues function as your event management team. Their job is to come together and meet or exceed the expectations you created at the point of sale.

If you collectively adopt a culture of serving others, the primary focus is on delivering exceptional customer service both internally and externally. It puts customers at the heart of your business and takes precedence over personal gains.

A servant culture breaks down internal silos and divisions that sometimes exist within companies.

By getting this right, you can cultivate a regular stream of loyal, repeat customers, and also ones who promote your business through positive word of mouth, social media, and favourable online reviews. The customers will be marketing your services on your behalf.

New buyers who have been referred by your customers are particularly valuable, as they are more likely to trust your abilities and be less price-sensitive than those who haven't received a personal recommendation.

Buyers Are Value Extractors

To effectively stage an event, it's important to understand how buyers make their purchasing decisions. Although price is a factor, buyers are typically focused on achieving maximum value from their investment. They are value extractors.

Numerous factors will contribute to their perception of value and success. When the benefits of doing business with you are perceived to outweigh the costs, buyers are more likely to make a purchase.

Here's a practical example of how buyers will choose *perceived value* over price.

Two nightclubs sit side by side, both offering live music, appealing decor, and well-stocked bars. However, one of them appears lacklustre and is half-empty while the other is thriving, with a long queue waiting to be allowed inside.

Surprisingly, the second nightclub charges an entry fee at the door and offers more expensive refreshments. The question that arises is why individual buyers are willing to queue up and pay more when they could pay less and get the same thing with no delays, right next door.

The answer lies in the *perceived value* they expect to extract from paying the cover charge and for higher drink prices. Their expectation is that the band will be better, they will be safer, the ambience and service will be top-notch, and they will be mixing with the 'right' crowd. If the night out meets their expectations, they will consider it money well spent. If dissatisfied, they will feel aggrieved and disappointed.

What Buyers Want

When a potential buyer is considering a purchase, there will generally be more than one key value driver that forms the basis of their evaluation and selection process. Here are the most common ones.

Price – Buyers will pay more if you demonstrate either the lowest overall cost solution or the perception of excellent value for money. You can be competitive without being cheap.

Time – Buyers want minimal time commitment, both before and after making their purchase. They want a supplier who takes responsibility and doesn't need micromanaging.

Extras – Buyers want transparency, where the quoted price reflects the actual purchase cost without unexpected add-on charges emerging later in their purchasing process.

Effort – Buyers want a pain-free relationship. This means you prioritise their needs and they can trust you to take the initiative and communicate potential issues before they arise.

Risk – Buyers are risk averse. They do not want to take on unnecessary risks or expose themselves to the emotional and financial consequences of making a bad purchasing decision.

Staging Successful Events

The formula for salespeople to be in the event management business is a simple one: understand the buyer's needs, find a point of difference, create an event, and then 'stage' the perception of an experience.

Here are three highly effective tactics that, if adopted, will help you stand out and set your events apart.

1. *Value For Money*

First and foremost, let's address the issue of pricing and value for money. It's important your buyers understand there's a substantial difference between the initial invoice price they pay for their purchase and the cost. The upfront price is merely the starting point. The real cost won't be determined until later and can extend throughout the entire lifespan of the product or service.

Every purchase entails a combination of both known and unknown costs. Once you grasp this equation, even if your price is higher than your competitors, you can confidently educate your buyers and showcase your services as the best value for money or the lowest overall cost solution. Here's the formula for differentiating a cost from a price.

Invoice Price + Product Defects + Service Errors = Actual Cost

Known costs include the seller's invoice price and published add-on prices.

Unknown costs could include price blowouts, purchase not being fit for purpose, service failure, product defect, subpar warranty, poor communication and timekeeping, security issues, and the financial stability of the seller.

Here's a straightforward example of how factoring in unknown costs can influence a purchasing decision. Let's consider a scenario where a buyer is in the market for a car.

The sticker prices on vehicles displayed in a dealer's yard represent the upfront cost of the purchase. The *real* cost includes not only the purchase price, but also the unpredictable future cost of fuel, insurance, maintenance, and repairs. Additionally, there are potential future emotional burdens tied to factors like parts availability and recurring breakdowns.

When these unknown future costs are taken into account, a cheap gas-guzzler with limited dealer support will often be considered less cost-effective than a newer, more expensive, fuel-efficient model from a reputable dealer.

2. Win the Moments of Truth

> "The opportunity to defeat the enemy is provided by the enemy himself."
>
> ~ Sun Tzu, *The Art of War*

Moments of truth are the points and/or interactions with a brand when consumer perceptions of that brand are established. Essentially, each time there's an interaction, it represents a moment of truth.

In 2011, Google coined the term *zero moments of truth*. This refers to the research consumers conduct about a product or service before any contact is even initiated. If you lose a zero moment of truth, it means you have been eliminated before their purchasing journey even starts.

As a salesperson, the moments of truth you need to be concerned about are the ones that dictate your buyer's evaluation and selection process. From the first moment you connect with them, every interaction is an opportunity to win that moment.

If you can stay in process and extend the buyer's purchasing journey, you will often find yourself as the last one standing, or the only logical choice. That's because your competitors will organically eliminate themselves by any of the following.

- Limited capability
- Poor communication
- Lack of genuineness
- Being overly transactional
- Poor timekeeping
- Overselling
- Lack of follow-up
- General tardiness

In essence, through progressive relationship building and aligning your approach to the buyer's purchasing journey, you can defeat your enemies (competitors) and win the buyer's order without a fight.

3. Paint Histories of the Future

The ability to paint your buyers a 'history of their future' is one of the most powerful skills in your sales toolkit. It is also the primary method for staging a successful event.

To begin, it's important to discover and understand the practical and emotional needs of your buyer. Once you have a thorough appreciation of their needs, it's essential to shift your focus towards their desired future. By doing this, you can develop your solution by using the end-user experience as your starting point and then working backward to the present.

While it's important to consider the practical and technical aspects of your solution, this is secondary to understanding the vision and the emotional connection it will deliver.

The key to your value proposition therefore lies in creating a compelling mental image and emotional connection to the buyer's desired future. Remember that simplicity and clarity are crucial; you don't need to delve into the complexity or intricate details of your plan until you become their preferred choice or have already been selected as their service provider. This approach is not only effective in sales but is also applicable to various aspects of our everyday decision-making.

Here is a practical example. A sports team's first meeting of the season is generally used to define the team's goals and what they want to achieve. They use powerful imagery to envision a positive future, what a successful season looks like, and how that will make them feel. Things like holding up the winners' cup, public recognition, and earning financial rewards are all part of their vision.

These mental pictures serve as powerful motivators and drivers for the team, inspiring them to strive towards their goals. The initial stage is focused on the end result rather than the specifics of how they will achieve it. That comes later.

In our personal lives, the technique of painting our 'history of the future' can also be used to solve both simple and complex personal concerns. It takes us beyond the complexity of our issue to a place of clarity. We visualise what a successful future both looks and feels like.

Once we understand the future, the steps to achieving our desired outcome become more apparent. The timing of our solution can then be planned and timetabled from the future back to the present.

Key Takeaways

Irrespective of what industry or business you are in, if you're a sales professional, you're also in the event management business. Your challenge is to set the scene for your buyers, as tangible benefits will only materialise after a purchase is made.

This requires that the events you create, and stage must generate excitement and the expectation of a positive end-user experience, both practically and emotionally. Remember, buyers are value extractors. When perceived benefits exceed perceived costs, value is created and purchasing decisions are made.

Chapter Three:
Sales Velocity = More Sales

Sales velocity is the measurement of how quickly a buyer moves through your sales process. The basic concept is that the less time this takes, the faster you can close more deals and thus generate more revenue.

Improving sales velocity is one of the easiest ways of converting more potential buyers into paying customers. Most salespeople want to close more sales within a shorter time period.

Velocity selling offers a great deal of flexibility, which is one of its main advantages. It can be used as a technique in specific situations, or as a comprehensive strategy implemented throughout a company. When used as a strategy, it is particularly effective for businesses that generate large volumes of inbound leads from click-throughs and phone inquiries.

Seasonal businesses can also leverage velocity selling during peak periods and then slow things right down during off-peak periods.

The Sales Velocity Formula

Sales velocity is calculated within specific time periods, as follows.

$$\text{Velocity} = (\text{\# of opportunities} \times \$ \text{ Value} \times \text{closing \%}) \:/ \text{ number of days to close}$$

The number of opportunities is the qualified leads that are generated. The dollar value is the total dollar value of the qualified leads, and the closing percentage is the number of qualified leads divided by the number won, which gives a percentage. The number of days to close is the average length of the sales cycle from receiving the lead to closing the sale.

Before your eyes glaze over, it's important to note that this formula can easily be calculated within most sales systems, or even manually. What's more important than the formula is how velocity selling can help you close more sales and generate more revenue in a shorter timeframe. Here's a simplified way of calculating what velocity can do for your sales output.

If you reduce the time it takes to convert a buyer into a customer by 50 percent, you will have 50 percent more time to repeat the process. This means that if you consistently achieve the same success rate, your sales revenue will double. Even if your closing percentage decreases by 30 percent, your sales revenue will still increase by 40 percent.

Velocity Selling 101

Here are some important tips to assist you on your velocity selling journey.

> To achieve sustainable success, you must bring your colleagues along for the journey.

Velocity selling is a team effort

Velocity selling has great benefits but if it's put in the hands of individual salespeople without support, you can lose a lot of money very quickly.

If you fly solo as a velocity seller, you will eventually start cutting corners and be battling for bookings, margin – and cooperation from your own colleagues.

Velocity selling isn't about short-circuiting your sales process. It's about accelerating the speed your whole team can move buyers through the stages of their purchasing journey. It doesn't matter if *they* skip steps, as long as *you* don't.

Unless you are an owner-operator or work in a very small business, there are multiple variables and team inputs that you and your sales team cannot manage or control on your own. These can include the number of leads generated, type of lead, deal size, technology applications, operational capability, customer culture, and many others.

To achieve sustainable success, you must bring your colleagues along for the journey.

This entails using your sales skills to overcome internal obstacles and persuade everyone involved to accelerate their processes and adopt a more buyer-centric approach. It begins with the marketing team and the quality of leads they generate and extends to your service delivery teams, who may need to handle short-notice bookings or go the extra mile.

The law of diminishing intent

The law of diminishing intent is the enemy of velocity selling. It effectively means that if a buyer is interested in what you have to offer, the longer they delay in making the purchase, the less likely they are to follow through with it.

There could be any number of reasons for this. They may lose focus. New competitors can emerge from the woodwork. Or they may get frustrated by the process and just make a random purchasing decision to get it over with.

Prioritise new enquiries

Velocity selling, as a strategy, is effective if you have a mindset and process that prioritises new enquiries over potential buyers already in the pipeline. The idea is to move new buyers as far as possible through your sales process before turning your attention to the next immediate opportunity. The faster you respond to a new enquiry, the more sales you can make – without competition or without a fight. If there's a genuine possibility of taking a fresh enquiry straight through your process to a firm booking, it's essential to single-mindedly push forward until you close that opportunity.

A good habit is to reserve the mornings for taking inbound leads as they come in, particularly digital leads that were generated overnight. Start with the first lead of the day (unless there's something particularly important that needs doing). As your day progresses, there will be ample time in the afternoon to follow up on your pending proposals or connect with other buyers already in the pipeline.

Be quick – don't hurry

Velocity selling doesn't entail disregarding your established sales process. Rather, it requires you and your colleagues to reduce the overall time it takes to effectively turn buyers into customers. Below are some effective techniques and tips for velocity selling.

- Go bone-deep. Uncover the real needs of your buyers, not just the obvious ones. The velocity of their purchasing decisions will be significantly increased if you can find the perfect solution to both known and hidden needs.

- Build trust and velocity with buyers by maintaining frequent communication and setting up appointments for the next step, even if it's just to respond to a question within the next ten or fifteen minutes.

- Don't collaborate with buyers. Keep your thoughts to yourself while you uncover their real needs and find solutions that work. This prevents them from normalising your expertise and using it to educate competitors. It also enables you to deliver a positive surprise when the time comes to close the sale.

- Velocity-led solutions are built around each individual buyer's vision of their future. How your solution resonates and makes them feel is just as important as the practical aspects. It will have a significant impact on the speed of their decision-making.

Optimise the whole sales cycle

Velocity selling requires tweaking everything around your sales process to reduce time-wasting and inefficiencies. This could involve the incorporation of additional automated processes within the sales cycle. Or perhaps developing a new range of templated sales proposals that are easy for buyers to understand and sign off on. For instance, you can limit free text fields and introduce abbreviated, easy-to-read terms and conditions.

One important aspect of velocity selling is to prioritise effectiveness over efficiency. Whenever possible, use phone and text communication rather than relying on long email threads and waiting for replies. This applies to both internal and external communication.

Using a text system with automated non-reply messaging can be an effective prompt for buyers to phone you, which is exactly what you want to happen. Maximising phone time is all-important to a velocity seller. That's because you must not only stay in touch with your buyers, but also spend an equal amount of time discussing arrangements with your internal service delivery teams.

Generate urgency and scarcity

For velocity sellers, there are two ingredients that make all the difference. These are urgency and scarcity.

Buyers tend to take action and make purchases when they perceive a limited availability or capacity. The introduction of either of these factors into your buyer's psyche is particularly effective if you operate in a sector that practices variable or dynamic pricing.

For example, an effective strategy is to pencil-book the necessary resources for a booking before presenting your proposal to a buyer. By offering a solution that meets their needs while guaranteeing both supply and perfect timing, you can also introduce urgency and scarcity into their decision-making. Pencil-booked resources should have a time limit, or sunset clause applied, giving the buyer a limited period to commit to your proposal. A sunset clause should have genuine reasons, for example, taking advantage of a special discounted price, or in this instance, guaranteeing supply by locking in essential resources and dates.

Compare yourself to yourself

A key velocity-selling strategy is to always compare yourself to yourself, not to your competitors. This is especially important when negotiating or offering a price incentive for booking early.

Your conversations with buyers should be built around the difference between what you normally charge in comparison to what you are offering. Don't enter into debates about competitors' prices for the same or similar services. By validating a competitor's business, you are handing control back to the buyer and run the risk of engaging in a price war.

At the very least, you will slow down the speed of your sales process. At the worst, you risk losing the sale.

If price remains an issue, focus the buyer on your proposal being the best overall cost solution, taking into account both known and unknown costs. The invoice or purchase price only gets them to the start line and your solution has minimal unknown costs and is supported by a compelling brand promise.

The Key Question that Needs Answering

At some point prior to presenting their buyer with a sales proposal, or value proposition, every velocity seller must ask the buyer this question:

"Under the right circumstances, are you in a position to make a decision?"

This can be challenging, even for experienced sellers. That's because it throws buyers off balance and can bring about a period of awkward silence. They will need a few seconds to recover and formulate their response.

The reason this question is crucial to a velocity-selling strategy is that it enables you to identify genuine active buyers from those who aren't prepared to make a decision.

A percentage of inactive buyers may even be positively activated by this question alone.

The reality is that if the buyer's velocity is not aligned to yours, any special insights or benefits you offer for a quick booking will almost certainly become benchmarks to be used against you.

It's advisable to ask this question before you present your proposal, but not during the same conversation. If the answer is yes, they are able to make a decision, then you have aligned their velocity to yours.

Let them know you will be back to them very quickly with your proposal. The shorter the time period between asking the question, receiving an affirmation, and presenting your proposal, the more velocity you can generate.

As a suggestion, it's recommended you introduce the question with a gentler opening statement, such as, "I'm working on a proposal I think you will really like."

If your buyer's response to the key question is vague or a flat-out no, it's important to understand the reason behind it. Ask a follow-up question, such as, "Can you share what's preventing you from making a decision?"

They may need to consult with a partner, in which case, you can inquire about their partner's availability to have that discussion. If the partner is available at short notice or overnight, you are now realigned. If there's no chance of a decision being made promptly, or if they're merely window-shopping, it's best to slow down and reduce the velocity of your approach, or you risk losing the sale.

Presenting Your Proposal – With Velocity

Ideally, pitch your value proposition verbally before putting it in writing. Emphasise the essential benefits and demonstrate how your solution meets both their practical and emotional needs.

This approach not only enables you to make last-minute adjustments, but it's also an opportunity to ask for the booking before it's formalised. If you pencil-book or pre-book the required resources for specific dates, you can move your buyer beyond the decision-making stage to a place where their choice has already been made. They may want to renegotiate the timing, but not their choice of service partner.

If the pencil-bookings are subject to a sunset clause, your buyer will naturally feel the pressure of time, making them more likely to make a decision under urgency.

After this conversation, it's crucial to have your formal proposal en route as quickly as possible. They will expect to see it in writing, and delays may cause them to doubt the professionalism of your approach.

A good tip is to text the buyer before pushing the 'send' button. This will generate additional velocity, alleviate concerns they may have about potential delays, and keep your proposal top of mind.

After allowing them enough time to read your proposal, follow up with urgency. They may have questions, want to negotiate, or need further encouragement to make a decision in your favour.

Key Takeaways

Incorporating velocity selling techniques into your sales process is a powerful way to increase sales revenue by reducing the time it takes to convert buyers into paying customers. It provides flexibility and can be used in various situations or as a stand-alone strategy across your company. It is especially beneficial for businesses with high volumes of inbound leads from click-throughs and phone inquiries.

Chapter Four:
How To Activate Buyers

All salespeople are routinely faced with timewasters and tire-kickers who have no genuine need or interest in their business. There are others who may be genuine but don't have the budget or require services that fall outside the company's parameters.

While many successful salespeople are adept at identifying and disengaging from these non-buyer types, there are others who get it wrong and eliminate genuine buyers based upon initial impressions and trying to qualify them by personality type.

Do First Impressions Count?

If you're in sales, relying on first impressions to evaluate a new buyer's potential is not a viable strategy. The reason for this is mainly due to the presence of both conscious and unconscious biases within us all. These can significantly impact our perceptions. As a result, we may inadvertently narrow our sales funnel by filtering out potential buyers we believe are unworthy.

Our *conscious biases* are beliefs and attitudes of which we are aware. A *conscious* bias can occur even before physical contact has been made. Here's an example.

In my previous life as a CEO, I was troubled by the high number of disqualified leads coming in from our company's digital inquiry forms. I discovered that the lead handling and sales teams were randomly rejecting inquiries from certain ethnicities.

I had to educate them that they were leaking a high percentage of potential new buyers before we had even met them. Their *conscious biases* were not only socially unacceptable, but also prevented us from moving the business forward.

Unconscious bias is more difficult to detect because it operates outside of our conscious awareness. It can stem from things like racial stereotyping, gender bias, age bias, LGBTQ+ bias, orientation bias, and social grouping bias. In sales, even the assumption that someone who is well-presented, well-groomed, and attractive is more financially competent and trustworthy than someone who isn't is a form of unconscious bias.

Does Personality Profiling Work?

The answer to the question does personality profiling work is yes and no. While it's true that personality profiling can help salespeople communicate better with certain buyers, it's unfortunate that many have turned personality profiling into an all-encompassing strategy.

After all, it's fun, exciting, and can be a great motivator at sales meetings, seminars, and conferences. As a result, many salespeople have replaced the fundamentals of selling with popularity contests based upon personality.

Even if successfully implemented, personality profiling can lead to unintended consequences, such as buyers selecting the best solution at the lowest price and then asking the seller they like the most to match both.

Some of the doubts around the reliability and accuracy of qualifying buyers by personality type can include the following.

- Is personality profiling just another form of stereotyping and social grouping?

- Can a salesperson successfully qualify an individual's personality type after just one interaction, when trained psychologists could take months to do the same thing?

- Does personality profiling identify the buyers who carefully disguise their true selves or become withdrawn when they meet a salesperson?

While it's important to note that personality profiling can be a useful tool in sales, it's not a one-size-fits-all approach and should only be used in combination with other techniques and strategies.

The Buyer Activation Blueprint

The process of activating buyers by category, not personality, is an effective and accurate way for sellers to position themselves for consistent success. This method is easy to understand, and most importantly, driven by the buyer, not the seller.

A buyer category refers to a grouping of buyers based upon their needs, timing, buying behaviour, and decision-making processes. The basis is that irrespective of their personality type or social grouping, most buyers embark on a similar purchasing journey.

- They have a need or problem that needs resolving.

- They conduct an information search to identify potential suppliers of the product or service they need.

- They initiate contact and evaluate the alternatives, including the cost of the purchase and the value they can extract for that cost.

- They make a purchasing decision.

While most buyers use similar purchasing processes, they don't all fall into the same grouping or category.

Once you've separated the genuine buyers from the timewasters, your role is to activate as many of them as possible. This entails transitioning them into a category where they are open to making a decision, preferably in favour of your services over others.

The Three Categories of Buyers

1. The Active Buyer

As a salesperson, your aim is to transition the maximum number of buyers into the category of active buyers. This is because active buyers are the ones who are motivated or can be motivated to make a purchase. They are open-minded and use a combination of logic and emotion to reach a decision.

If they are given the right messages or triggers, most active buyers can be motivated to abandon their planned purchasing journey and make a swift decision. For example, if they are dissatisfied with others they've met, an active buyer will sometimes choose the first seller who can demonstrate a genuine interest in their needs and how they can be of service.

Early in their relationship, one of the biggest issues for many sellers is the overwhelming desire to collaborate with buyers. If you share your knowledge too early in the sales process, many of the buyers who were initially receptive to making a quick decision will be deactivated, not activated. That's because your expertise and insights can easily be passed on to your competitors, allowing them to offer similar solutions and compete against you.

Your role isn't to educate buyers by sharing your skillsets and trade secrets. It is to understand their needs, uncover hidden needs, and then provide bespoke solutions that meet those needs, ultimately leading to a confirmed booking for your business.

2. The Status Quo Buyer

Because they are in no great hurry, the status quo buyer is the most difficult to deal with and activate. While some are procrastinators or pontificators, the majority are conducting research for something that won't happen until the distant future.

For instance, they may be researching the purchase of a new car. However, the timing will be determined by the expiry date on their existing warranty, in twelve months' time. Prospective sellers can only follow up with status quo buyers a certain number of times before they risk becoming an annoyance. In many cases, they will lose touch with these buyers and need to wait until the buyer is ready to contact them on their own terms.

For salespeople, the status quo buyer is the type who can easily be disregarded as a timewaster.

However, even the pontificators are genuine buyers, albeit at some point in the future. A strategy some sellers use is to slow things down by giving a price range for the future, not the present. The bottom end of this price range should be lower than the seller's current pricing. The top end should be higher. Buyers tend to look at the bottom of the range, not the top. This can keep their interest during the 'status quo' period.

Another strategy is to entice status quo buyers by presenting them with an appealing 'book now' price that remains valid for an extended time period. This ensures both availability and price, allaying their fear of missing out (FOMO) when they are ready to buy.

If you offer a special inflation-proof price and guaranteed supply, ask the buyer to lock in the deal by paying a deposit. The benefit for sellers is that they can build a base of guaranteed future business.

For salespeople, the status quo buyer is
the type who can easily be disregarded as
a time-waster.

A caveat: If the timeline is extended well into the distant future, there is a risk of lowering future margins due to cost increases.

3. The Spreadsheet Buyer

The spreadsheet buyer is not difficult for sellers to identify. They plan their purchasing journey in a practical, methodical, and mathematical manner. They cast a wide net and want to compare service providers on an apples-to-apples basis. They are also value extractors who search for differences.

To facilitate their decision-making, they often create a spreadsheet that directly compares prices and features across all options. These buyers enjoy negotiating and will regularly request their shortlisted sellers to match or outdo competitors' prices. Being methodical, their process for deciding may appear lengthy and long-winded.

Sales professionals aim to disrupt the rhythm of these buyers by introducing positive surprises and thoughtful differentiators that shift them into the active category. If they remain within the confines of their spreadsheets and analytical process, the likelihood of securing a favourable deal decreases significantly.

The key to activating spreadsheet buyers is to take them to a place where they grant themselves permission to make a purchase. Ultimately, it is emotions that will steer them away from their planned approach and into the active category.

Below are some of the strategies you can use to activate spreadsheet buyers.

- Uncover a silver bullet – an undisclosed issue or need – that you can address with a solution that delivers both practical and emotional benefits. If you initially withhold this information, you can prevent the buyer from sharing it with competitors while simultaneously creating an element of surprise. For maximum effect, reveal the need and proposed solution in a one-on-one discussion just prior to finalising your proposal. Try to incorporate an element of urgency and/or scarcity around your solution. This approach is intended to positively surprise the buyer and change their planned pathway.

- Focus them on the emotional aspect of their purchasing decision. One way you can achieve this is by painting mental pictures of how they will feel once your solution has been implemented. Emotions are often tied to family, work, health, social status, personal interests, or material possessions. As an example, a buyer searching for a new home has visited numerous open houses and viewings without finding the right fit. A savvy seller discovers that their ultimate goal is to move in before Christmas, and subsequently introduces them to a selection of vacant properties. The seller triggers the buyer's emotions and motivates them into making the purchase by painting a mental picture of the family being comfortably settled in their new home, surrounded by their cherished possessions, and enjoying a delightful Christmas dinner.

- You can appeal to the logical and intelligent side of the spreadsheet buyer by highlighting the potential consequences of making a wrong decision. The emphasis is on your solution being the smartest choice. Spreadsheet buyers appreciate being considered as astute and intelligent. You could emphasise your brand promise and the benefits of having a product or service guarantee that extends beyond superficial assurances. If it's a significant purchase, you can highlight the lifetime value of your solution, rather than the initial upfront cost. Specific examples should be given to illustrate the benefits. The core premise is to persuade them that not purchasing from you could be an expensive mistake both financially and emotionally.

Key Takeaways

While there are many outstanding sales gurus and trainers with countless methods of personality profiling, my experience is that these are primarily conversation pieces and time-fillers for sales meetings and seminars. Profiling individual personalities is best left to trained professionals who can take months or even years to accomplish the same objective. If you can set aside your biases and focus on identifying the category your buyer belongs to, you can employ tried and tested sales techniques to transition genuine buyers into the active category. This is where the magic happens for both you and the buyer.

Chapter Five:
Clarity Lives Beyond Complexity

In all aspects of our lives, clarity lives on the far side of complexity. Clarity in our day-to-day interactions is about communicating in a way that is coherent, clear, and concise. Clarity promotes understanding, which is crucial in both interpersonal and business interactions.

Complexity refers to the quality of being intricate, detailed, or difficult to understand. A good example of complexity is the terms and conditions we often tick without reading when we enter into a commercial transaction.

Clarity vs Complexity in Sales

The goal of all salespeople is to consistently win profitable business. To accomplish this, it's necessary to resonate and make a lasting impression with buyers. It all starts with listening carefully to the buyer's voice, communicating in a clear manner, and avoiding the overuse of technical terms and industry jargon.

Nothing unravels a sales opportunity faster than complexity. That's because buyers can easily be distracted by their personal situations, convoluted sales processes, and overly technical specifications. If salespeople try to sell in an overly detailed manner, this approach can lead to breakdowns in communication – and lost sales. It's crucial for salespeople to keep their messaging clear, simple, straightforward, and easy to understand.

Quarter-inch Drill or Quarter-inch Hole?

One of my favourite marketing quotes is attributed to renowned economist and former Harvard Business School Professor Theodore Levitt.

> "People don't want to buy a quarter-inch drill; they want a quarter-inch hole!"
>
> ~ Theodore Levitt

This quote reminds us about the importance of understanding the buyer's real needs and applying the perfect solution to their problem. In this context, the quarter-inch hole represents their end goal or desired outcome.

It's important for the seller to focus on the quarter-inch hole rather than promoting the features of what drill they will use and how they will go about drilling the hole. They are selling the benefits of their solution, not the fine detail of how they will accomplish the task.

Simplicity is Clarity's Best Friend

In sales, simplicity and clarity are best friends. Having clarity creates an environment for simplicity. That's because simple and straightforward messages that strike a chord with potential buyers are more likely to be understood and acted upon.

It's important to note that simplicity should not be mistaken for being simplistic. When we are simplistic, we manage problems in a manner that is superficial and reliant upon our preconceived notions and prejudices. Being simplistic is a state that exists on the near side of complexity, where the thought process and focus is overly simple and skin-deep.

For example, if we encounter a buyer who appears to be fixated on price, we may ignore going through our usual discovery process and offer them the cheapest option that's available. In reality, the lowest overall cost solution for that individual may be a higher-priced option due to its lifetime value and the emotional benefits it can provide, which surpass the invoice price.

Simplicity, in contrast, is something completely different.

The Apple iPhone, an icon in its own right, serves as a prime illustration of simplicity in design, usability, construction, and features. Since its inception in 2007, the iPhone has led the way in the worldwide transition to mobile computing and cellular phones. The consistency and simplicity of design have been embedded in the DNA of the iPhone. Despite the flashy and feature-packed alternatives provided by its competitors, every new iPhone release continues to be a significant and celebrated global event.

Unconscious Bias Is Clarity's Enemy

We all rely on mental shortcuts, beliefs, and perspectives to help us make sense of the world. These can sometimes make us misinterpret things without realising it. This is known as *unconscious bias*, which can lead to prejudice against specific genders, age groups, races, religions, communities, or individuals. If clarity and simplicity are a seller's friend, then unconscious biases are the enemy.

In both sales and life situations, our unconscious bias can seriously hinder our decision-making abilities by subverting the facts without our awareness. This can involve disregarding evidence or situations that contradict our individual beliefs, displaying favouritism towards certain personalities, or making hasty assessments and either overlooking or ignoring other essential information.

For instance, if you are dealing with a buyer you perceive to be grumpy, arrogant, or overly transactional, it can be easy to unconsciously exclude them from your normal sales process. This could include neglecting to ask important questions, avoiding one-on-one contact, or missing important sales steps.

In actual fact, they could just be having a difficult day. Maybe they're preoccupied with other issues, or simply being cautious while they evaluate your performance.

How To Eliminate Your Biases

In all sales situations, it's important to double-check your own thought process and identify any biases you may have in play. By asking yourself a few questions, you can quickly identify – and eliminate – any unhelpful beliefs and assumptions that otherwise may go undetected. Here are some questions to ask yourself.

- Have I stereotyped or made negative assumptions about a buyer without attempting to better understand their situation or substantiate these assumptions?

- Am I gravitating to or overly attracted to a buyer? Am I short-circuiting my usual process, believing the attraction is mutual and I've already won the business?

- Prior to planning my approach, have I researched the known facts and discussed my findings with a colleague who has no 'skin in the game' or biases?

Designing Solutions That Sell

If you take the initiative to eliminate your biases and integrate clarity and simplicity into your sales approach, you will reap the benefits. Your sales pipeline will have less leakage, and your value propositions will be clearer, unambiguous, and more persuasive. This will not only result in an increased volume of bookings, but also a rise in satisfied customers and the potential for more referral business in the future.

By incorporating the following three self-management techniques into your sales strategy, you will gain a deeper insight into your own thoughts and be able to accurately identify effective sales solutions. By doing so, you can confidently prepare and present your buyers with clear and persuasive value propositions that resonate and produce results.

Step 1 - Understand

> Use your insights later, when it's time to
> win their business.

Seek first to understand. Irrespective of what sales method you follow, your first step should always be to meet with your buyer, either face-to-face, by phone, or video call. This is where you identify what you need to be clear about by asking open questions of them and yourself.

Your focus is on their needs, not what you want to achieve. Keep in mind that buyers can rarely state specifically what their real needs are. To identify these, you may have to delve deeper to challenge their thinking and, if necessary, reshape their thoughts and opinions.

Ideally, any challenges should be actioned retrospectively by calling back and reopening the discussion on specific points.

During your first buyer meeting, avoid the temptation to voice your opinions. Your job isn't to make them experts. Use your insights later, when it's time to win their business.

Step 2 - Visualise

Visualisation isn't complicated. We all do it to some degree. It's a way of mentally rehearsing and experiencing what we want in life.

In this context, it's about ignoring the complexity of your buyer's purchasing journey by mentally rehearsing what you want them to experience as a result of their purchase. The actual technique is to set yourself a mental picture of what their desired future looks like and how that will make them feel. As you should already be aware of what they *think* they need, you can either visualise that reality or an alternative future based upon any hidden needs you have uncovered.

It's important to understand that during your initial meeting, many buyers will have either ignored or disregarded the emotional component of their needs. This is why your visual picture will be focused on how you want them to *feel*, in addition to the practical aspects.

Step 3 – Create the pathway

After achieving clarity around the buyer's desired future, it's time to organize your thoughts by planning a pathway from that point back to the present day. You will need to incorporate specific details like the sequence of events, timing, resource allocation, and third-party involvement.

After determining your solution is workable, you are now in a position to bring it to life by preparing your value proposition. The key components will include:

- a clear understanding of their real needs and desired future

- an unambiguous pathway to that future

- a solution that is user-friendly, easy to describe, and fit for purpose

When pitching your value proposition, the primary focus should be on playing it backwards, from the future back to the present. You do this by painting them a compelling 'history of their future,' the same mental pictures you have already visualised and rehearsed on their behalf.

Key Takeaways

Regardless of whether you are strategising your own life or identifying and addressing the needs of your buyers', clarity and simplicity will always be found beyond complexity, not on the near side. By adopting these simple techniques and approaching your sales solutions from the future back to the present day, you can avoid the pitfalls of preparing value propositions that don't resonate and are either overly simplistic or too complicated.

Chapter Six:
Discovering Sales Discovery

In sales, the term *discovery* refers to the process of gathering important information from potential buyers in order to understand their needs, challenges, and goals. While other terms like *needs assessment* or *needs analysis* are also used, *discovery* best captures the essence of the activity.

Discovery is a critical part of most sales processes because it enables sellers to gather valuable insights that will form the basis of their value proposition. The discovery process helps establish strong rapport and trust between buyers and sellers.

The Sales Discovery Meeting

The goal of a sales discovery meeting is to gain a comprehensive understanding of each potential buyer's unique situation and gather detailed information about their needs. A successful meeting will also uncover hidden needs and pain points they don't even know they have.

As the seller, your role is to ask questions, listen carefully to the buyer's responses, and gain an understanding of their perspective. The insights they share become the foundation of your solution, enabling you to prepare a value proposition that will both resonate and address their specific needs.

A sales discovery meeting between yourself and a potential buyer is most effective when it's a stand-alone meeting, either in person, over a videoconferencing platform, or by phone. Unless absolutely necessary, it shouldn't be conducted over email exchanges or by text messaging.

In many sales scenarios, you will already have the buyer's personal information, including the correct spelling of their name, phone number, why and how they contacted you, and a brief description of what they're looking to purchase. However, there are situations where you need to both collect this information and conduct a discovery meeting at the same time. This will be more effective if you treat these two functions separately, starting with the collection of vital information and then moving onto the discovery session.

Core Interpersonal Skills

A quality discovery meeting is about forming an alliance between yourself and the buyer. You need to be relaxed, open, and conversational while also probing the buyer with key questions and follow-up questions.

On the surface, the key requirements seem simple enough; you ask the right questions, and then actively listen to their responses.

Nevertheless, many salespeople struggle with this crucial part of the sales process. That's because they tend to lose interest if they aren't the ones speaking, and listen to respond rather than to understand. Some are overly confident and believe they have all the answers before asking any questions, while others rush through or gloss over their questions so they can get to their sales pitch.

Here are some of the core interpersonal skills you can deploy to set the tone for a positive and successful discovery meeting.

Warmth – In this context, having warmth is about demonstrating kindness and acceptance, without any implication of being in an overly personal relationship.

Empathy – Having empathy involves acknowledging another person's perspective and view of the world. You must be willing to step into their shoes, experience their reality, and verbalise it back to them.

Respect – To demonstrate respect, it's important to put aside your personal perspectives and biases while acknowledging and appreciating those of the buyer. This approach can help you build trust and rapport without revealing your own opinions and differences.

Genuineness – Genuineness is crucial in building trust and rapport with potential buyers. Focus on being authentic, sincere, and attentive to their needs. Avoid misleading buyers or pressuring them into a purchase that doesn't align with their requirements.

Meeting Planning and Preparation

Practice the Five P's

Prior preparation prevents poor performance.

This is an adage that could just as easily be *fail to plan, plan to fail*. Both quotes suggest that if you want to perform well or succeed in a task, you must take the time to prepare beforehand.

This preparation includes things like research, planning, and practice, while also allocating sufficient time so you're not in a rush either before or after the meeting.

Here are some tips to help you plan and prepare for a sales discovery meeting.

- Find a quiet place to do your preparation. Review what you know and think through your interview plan and questions. In some situations, this won't be possible, so have a generic list committed to memory. Bear in mind that your initial questions are just to get the ball rolling. Start with some easy ones, like confirming their basic details, correct spelling, etc. Then graduate to more challenging open-ended questions.

- It's good practice to prepare in advance for any potential objections or concerns the buyer may unexpectedly raise. While discovery meetings should always focus on the buyer and their needs, it's possible they may not follow the script and come out of left field with an unexpected question or raise their own premeditated objections.

- If you're calling a potential buyer without an appointment, start the conversation by asking if they have a few minutes to answer some questions. If they appear flustered or short of time, set an appointment to call back when it's convenient. Suggest a time that's soon, for example, in the next 15 or 30 minutes.

- When planning to meet in a home, office, or work environment, it's important to either prearrange a meeting room or quickly scan the venue to find a suitable spot in real time. It's best to sit at right angles to the buyer or around an oval-shaped meeting table, not face-to-face or in front of or behind an office desk. Off-site discovery meetings shouldn't be arranged in informal environments such as cafes or restaurants.

Open Questions and Probing Questions

As a salesperson, the most important discovery skill you need is the ability to ask open questions and probing questions. Open questions are used to gather information and establish rapport, and there are no right or wrong answers.

By way of explanation, an open question is one that can't be answered with a yes or no. It should encourage the other person to share their thoughts and feelings on a topic in their own words.

Consider the tone you would use when asking open-ended questions. Imagine a scenario in which you speak with a near neighbour who has unexpectedly put their family home on the market.

Some of the open questions you might ask include: Why are you selling? Where are you moving to? What sort of work will you be doing? When are you hoping to move? What does your partner think about the move? Where will the children go to school? As you can see, if you were to fire these questions at your neighbour without any context, it would quickly come across as aggressive and overwhelming.

It would be important, therefore, to adopt a tone that is both supportive and enthusiastic while also conveying a sense of loss, as they are moving away from the neighbourhood. There should be no implied criticism or negativity.

Probing questions are highly targeted and aim to delve deeper into a topic, helping the salesperson gain a better understanding of the buyer's perspective or situation. As a result, they encourage buyers to reflect more deeply, and often elicit more thoughtful responses.

A probing question is most effectively deployed as a follow-up to an open one. They typically start with words like, "Can you tell me more about..." "What specifically..." or, "How did that make you feel?"

When asking probing questions, keep in mind that your goal is to clarify the buyer's situation, not to interrogate or educate them.

Questioning Techniques

Questioning is a crucial aspect of effective communication, and there are numerous techniques and frameworks available to help make it easier. One of the most widely used and straightforward is the Five W's: What, When, Where, Why, and Who. These are interrogative words that can't be answered with a simple yes or no.

The Five W's technique is a straightforward yet powerful questioning approach. Once you're comfortable with the framework, it becomes easy to remember the sequence and use it to guide your conversations with buyers. Each question creates a logical thread to the next one, which may be more probing.

There is another questioning technique known as TEDS, which stands for tell, explain, describe, and show. This technique is also easy to remember and can be deployed either as a stand-alone method or in conjunction with the Five W's.

The TEDS method is more advanced than the Five W's and can be highly effective in capturing a buyer's attention and focus. Critical pieces of information can sometimes be uncovered with just one question.

The only issue with TEDS is that in their raw form, the questions can lead to short, stilted conversations. Try using a softer approach such as, *"Can you tell me a little more about that?"* This is preferable to a more demanding tone like, "Tell me more about that."

By using TEDS appropriately, you can engage the buyer in a more in-depth conversation and gain a better understanding of their needs and concerns.

The Big Discovery Meeting No-No's

Discovery meetings with potential buyers are critical for collecting information, gaining perspective, and achieving clarity on their needs and situation. However, certain common mistakes can prevent you from achieving your objectives and work against you. These big no-no's include, but are not limited to, the following.

- Talking about yourself and redirecting the conversation away from the buyer to promote your own beliefs and insights. If you focus on the buyer and their perspectives, you will be well on the way to building trust and genuine rapport. The time to highlight your talent will come later in the sales process.

- Filling in any gaps or silences in the conversation by overtalking. Remember that while you may have thought through your interview plan beforehand, your buyer is hearing your questions for the first time. They may need a moment to gather their thoughts before providing a response. By overtalking, you may inadvertently take this opportunity away from them. Silence can sometimes be golden.

- Avoid making leading statements that are assumptive and transparent with respect to your intentions. Being pushy, having biases for or against any individual or social group, and assuming you already know exactly what your buyer needs can quickly erode their trust and damage the relationship you are trying to build.

- Don't stack your questions on top of each other or machine-gun them at potential buyers with no genuine warmth or empathy. Your objective is to have quality conversations. This requires a conversational tone, active listening on your part, and a seamless progression from one question to the next.

Closing the Discovery Meeting

We talked earlier about opening a trust account and making a deposit. The discovery meeting is the perfect place for this to occur. Before closing a discovery meeting, simply make a promise – and then keep it. It can be as easy as sending them a link to specific information they will find informative. This should be unbiased, and not framed as part of your future sales pitch.

To ensure a smooth and effective close to a discovery meeting, there are some key steps that should help you to keep advancing your position and increase the likelihood of a successful outcome.

1. Summarise what you have learnt from the buyer and confirm your understanding of their needs.

2. Give them an opportunity to correct or clarify your understanding and ask further questions.

3. Most importantly, don't end the meeting without confirming the next course of action.

4. Within 24 hours of the meeting, you can further strengthen the buyer's confidence in you by sending a thank-you email or text message, summarising any commitments made and reconfirming the timing of your next actions.

Something important to remember is that when you establish a timeframe or set the appointment for your next buyer interaction, make sure you're a little vague about the purpose. The buyer may assume this is for you to either send or formally present your final proposal, but you may have other plans.

For example, you may want to challenge their perspective or discuss fresh insights that you've held back. You may have even uncovered a 'silver bullet' that will positively surprise them and help to close the sale.

Key Takeaways

Regardless of the sales process or methodology you subscribe to, acquiring the skills and knowledge to effectively plan and conduct a discovery meeting is one of the most pivotal steps you can make on your sales journey. It enables you to truly understand your buyers, uncover their real needs, and tailor your approach accordingly. By investing the necessary time and effort to thoroughly study and apply these techniques into your everyday sales interactions, you are taking significant strides towards achieving consistently positive outcomes.

Chapter Seven:
Sales Methods Made Easy

Sales methods can be confusing. There are so many different approaches and strategies out there. Successful salespeople often have their own unique style and approach, and there's a wide variance in what's considered a strategy, method, or process. This makes it challenging for businesses and salespeople to determine the best approach for their needs.

One thing most successful salespeople have in common is that they adopt a structured approach and prefer a simple, effective, and reliable sales system.

What is a Sales Method?

In general terms, a sales method is a framework or philosophy that companies and salespeople adopt to guide their sales process. Sales methodologies are more strategic than operational and aren't unique to any one organization. Many are universally known and can be applied across a wide range of companies and industry sectors.

Sales methods shouldn't be confused with sales processes. They are different, but also closely related. Sales *methods* are the overarching framework or philosophy that guide your sales approach, while sales *processes* are the repeatable series of steps and actions you adopt within that framework.

Most sales processes are unique and designed specifically for their own business. Two competing companies in the same market may have the same sales methodology but completely different sales processes.

Triple Threat Sales Methods

With so many sales methods out there, it can be difficult to choose the right one. Ultimately, the key to successful selling is to find a sales method that best fits your company's goals, your product or service, your target audience, and your individual strengths as a salesperson. You may even choose to vary your approach on a case-by-case basis.

Here are the strengths and weaknesses of three different sales methods that are in everyday use, either knowingly or unintentionally.

Transactional Selling

Transactional selling is a reactionary selling method. The salesperson cedes control to the buyer and applies a tactical approach within that framework.

It's reactionary because contact is generally initiated by the buyer, not the seller. The buyer appears to know what they want. There's the perception of a known problem and a known solution. The salesperson accepts this perception and focuses on making the transaction.

This method of selling is often deployed in low involvement, high volume, and/or high velocity situations.

It is ideally suited for call centres and 'click to buy' shopping where the efficiency and ease of the transaction can be a bigger selling point than the purchase itself. Straightforward purchases do not require complex sales methods.

In transactional selling, value is usually defined by the price and availability of the product or service. Some transactional buyers spend long hours researching their purchase on the internet. They make contact with their preferred sellers deep into their buying process. They see the salesperson's job as helping them buy something they have already picked.

Others will contact multiple sellers and make apples-to-apples comparisons. These buyers generally don't place a high value on the role of the salesperson, preferring to interact by email or text messaging. They ask direct questions and prefer short answers. As they are looking to get the best deal, many like to negotiate and may forfeit certain features to reduce their costs.

Transactional selling methods are more tactical than strategic. They can be deployed at any stage of the buyer's purchasing journey. Transactional sellers should be prepared to negotiate and never hesitate to ask the buyer for their budget, price expectation, or feedback on a price they have given.

To make a sale, they may need to lower their price by either taking out components of their service, introducing an alternative option, or bundling more than one product or service together.

Alternatively, if there's a supply shortage, they can take control of the buyer by adopting a take-it-or-leave-it approach with a time limit (sunset clause) for confirming the booking. This can be a positive sales tactic as it turns around the power dynamic between buyer and seller while also guaranteeing supply within the expiry period.

Another tactic for winning longer term or future bookings is to offer a 'book now' price, subject to the payment of a deposit. By locking in a good price and certainty of supply at a future date, the transactional buyer is achieving their two most important objectives.

Consultative Selling

Consultative selling is a more strategic selling method. The salesperson assumes there are unknown problems, unknown solutions, and unknown costs. They then collaborate with the buyer and educate them by sharing their experience, insights, and knowledge. The focus is on working together to find the buyer's pain points and building solutions to address them.

The seller will eventually assemble a value proposition that clearly outlines the problem they are solving, the solution(s) they can provide, and the value it delivers.

This selling method sits at the higher end of the services business. That's because it relies on trust and credibility. The seller feels safe because they have either been referred to the buyer by a higher authority or are well known as a leading expert in their field. It is also used when complex situations require extensive research before the buyer's issues are understood and solutions identified.

The initial contact could be made by either the salesperson or the buyer, given that many of these opportunities will arise from a referral.

Here's the catch; the consultative seller takes on the role of being a trusted adviser. This means their advice is transparent and unencumbered, even if it leads the buyer in another direction or is used by them to educate other sellers.

Consultative selling is most effective when the actual consulting processes are a paid service. This is especially true for higher-level services, such as health checks, where consumers may lack the knowledge or skills to make informed health decisions. In these cases, they are forced to trust the experience and reputation of others.

For example, if you feel unwell, you pay a fee to consult your family doctor. The doctor may then refer you to a specialist for an in-depth, paid consultation. You may even pay another fee to return to your family doctor and discuss the diagnosis. If an operation is recommended, this would become another paid service, provided by a specialist.

Unless you operate in a specialised niche (such as health or professional services) or are recognized as the leading expert in your field, a consultative selling approach is not recommended. This method can be time-consuming, and easily overcomplicate what may be a straightforward sale.

As a salesperson, you may be tempted to impress buyers with your insights and knowledge, but beware: most buyers are value extractors, not creators. The more you educate them, the more they may feel empowered to commoditise the value of that information and use it to coach your competitors. This can result in buyers either moving on to the next seller or making decisions based solely on price.

Solution Selling (Recommended)

Solution selling is a strategic selling method that can be deployed in most sales situations. It is highly recommended, as it sits in the sweet spot between transactional and consultative selling.

While transactional selling is about closing the deal, and consultative selling is based upon collaboration, solution selling sits between the two. It is a problem-led method and aims to firstly uncover and then address the buyer's specific needs and pain points. You are looking to provide a personalised buying experience where the buyer feels understood, appreciated, and that you're addressing their specific needs.

One of the key advantages of solution selling is that it allows you (as the seller) to build your sales process around each individual buyer's purchasing journey and guide them on that journey, not try to fit them into your sales structure. By putting yourself in their shoes, you can effectively see the world from their perspective and gain a clear understanding of their needs and pain points.

> Solution selling is a recommended method for most sales situations.

Your primary focus is on the buyer's desired outcome and the problem they need solving, rather than simply trying to sell them a specific product or service. Each solution you provide will be customised to the buyer's unique situation and requirements.

A solution sale comes to life when both buyer and seller acknowledge the buyer's problem and mutually sign off on the seller's solution. Most buyers will initially engage with a seller using a logical or left-brain approach. They have done their research, feel they know what they want, and have a shortlist of prospective providers and a process for evaluating them.

The skill of solution selling is to progressively alter the buyer's purchasing pathway so they choose you. This is achieved by initially appealing to the buyer's logical self, then slowly moving them to their right-brain or emotional self.

This is where the magic happens. How the buyer *feels* will ultimately be the determining factor in making a solution sale. Their emotional self will give them permission to buy.

Solution Selling vs Consultative Selling

Here's an example. I recently needed some remedial painting at my home. I did the research and contacted three painters. The first visited (that day) to scope the job. He took over and gave me an expert, in-depth overview of the work I needed to do and the options I should consider. He did the talking and I asked the questions. He was a consultative seller, and I was left in no doubt that he was a master painter.

That evening, he forwarded me a very detailed quotation and a price of around $5,000.

The second painter visited a day later. It was a short visit, as I was now an expert and quickly outlined what I wanted. As we moved around the house, he listened carefully and asked questions. Towards the end of his visit, he challenged what I assumed was necessary; what was I trying to achieve, and did I actually want a completely new paint job or just remedial work? He also asked if he could save me money by using the original house paint that was stored in the garage. This was his silver bullet.

He later sent a clear and concise quote with far less detail than the first painter and a price of around $2,900. I chose this painter and cancelled the third home visit. This was a case of the consultative seller being completely outdone by a solutions-based approach.

Key Takeaways

The triple threat of sales methodologies or frameworks is generally considered to be either transactional, consultative, or solution selling. For the reasons explained above, the adoption of solution selling is recommended as a preferred methodology, as it sits in the sweet spot between the other two. It is a versatile method that can adapt to different buying scenarios, effectively combining the efficiency and process-led approach of transactional selling with the relationship-building and problem-solving style of the consultative seller.

Chapter Eight:
Sales Process = Sales Success

Having a structured process to follow is vital for any professional salesperson. Sales is no different than any other profession. As an example, you would be horrified if you flew on a commercial aircraft and the professional pilot was flying the plane on gut instinct, without a series of documented and well-rehearsed steps, guidelines, and checklists to guide their actions.

In essence, sales processes are a step-by-step blueprint that help sellers become more efficient while also making the purchasing experience more positive for their buyers. The objective is to guide them on their purchasing journey and ultimately convert them into paying customers.

While your sales processes should be well-defined, they also need to be flexible, as the length of each individual sales cycle can vary greatly. Depending on the buyer, this can range from a few minutes to weeks, months, or even years.

One key principle remains constant: each step of the sales process should align with the steps of the buyer's purchasing journey, not vice versa.

Why Sales Winners Stay In Process

The reason top performers prefer to follow a well-defined sales process is because it helps them to consistently close more deals and thus earn more money. By replicating the same sequence of successful steps over and over, they achieve better results.

Although their process remains the same, they have the flexibility to adjust their tactics and velocity within each step to meet the needs of individual buyers. Even though they work deal by deal, salespeople operating within a structured process can manage multiple deals simultaneously, know where each deal stands, and quickly identify any deals that have stagnated or stalled.

Top performers don't rest on their laurels. They are learners who regularly monitor and fine-tune their sales process. Technology has given today's buyers the power to research extensively and take control of their own purchasing journeys, often engaging with salespeople late in their own process. As a result, they now value human qualities like empathy, trust, and insightfulness over slick salesmanship and practical information.

Without a buyer-centric process, it becomes more difficult for sellers to have influence and positively differentiate themselves. In many instances, their role is now to empower buyers to purchase rather than sell to them.

Designing Your Own Sales Process

While the majority of sales methodologies are well-established, it's commonplace for salespeople to design their own unique sales process. The goal is to develop a series of repeatable steps that can consistently convert buyers into paying customers.

It's important to have a guiding philosophy or method underpinning your process. For instance, solution selling is widely regarded as one of the best sales approaches for meeting the universal needs of modern buyers.

Here are five tips you can use to design your own sales process.

1. Understand your buyer – Identify the characteristics, preferences, and behaviours of your target buyers. This information will help you design a sales process that resonates with their needs and motivations.

2. Map the buyer's journey – Identify the steps of their purchasing journey so you can align your sales process to that journey. You don't need to create this from scratch, as there are plenty of examples freely available on the internet.

3. Define your sales steps – Once you have mapped out the buyer's journey, define the steps or stages that will make up your sales process. This could include things such as qualifying the lead, needs analysis, presentation, and closing.

4. Flesh out your key deliverables – Identify the actions and deliverables that are required at each step of your process. This could include activities such as conducting research, arranging buyer meetings, designing your solutions, and pitching your value proposition.

5. Incorporate flexibility – Remember, the process is a framework you work from, but your tactics should be adaptable depending on different buyer types, their needs, timing, the availability of your product or service, and financial considerations.

When designing your own bespoke sales process, try to avoid unnecessary complexity so you can deploy it universally, in any situation, with any buyer. Once you're up and running, it's only the beginning. From then on, it's all about continuous improvement, analysing your performance, testing different tactics, and recognising any of the steps that either aren't necessary or aren't working.

Solution Sales Process

Solution selling can be a game-changer for salespeople who want to revamp or refresh their approach and improve their performance. It is very versatile and can be deployed by both product and service sellers.

By putting the focus on understanding the buyer's needs and offering tailored solutions that address those needs, solution sellers can set themselves apart from the competition. It's all about empowering the buyer and making them feel heard, valued, and understood.

A solution-based approach can result in a high percentage of buyers giving themselves permission to buy rather than feeling like they're being pushed into it by a salesperson.

Deploying the Solution Sales Process

Here's an example of a 5-step solution sales process for inbound salespeople.

Step One	Evaluate	• Identify the source campaign. • Qualify lead type and confirm vital information. • Either set an appointment for discovery or commence discovery.
Step Two	Discovery	• Ask buyer the right questions. • Visualise their perfect end game and how it will feel. • Establish needs and pain points. • Listen carefully and validate their feelings.
Step Three	Add Value	• Focus on visual picture of the buyer's perfect outcome. • Build trust and add value, use differentiation and appreciation. • Offer special insight, reveal unknown needs and pain points.
Step Four	Engage	• Engage buyer and introduce your solution. • Paint a visual picture of their future and how they will feel. • Take feedback. • Positive feedback ask for the order, pending your formal proposal.

		• Move quickly.
		• Finalise and present your proposal.
		• Follow up ASAP.
Step Five	Commit	• Refresh proposal and negotiate if necessary. Alternatively ask for permission to proceed and sign the contract.

Step 1 – Evaluate

The initial step of this process entails screening and disqualifying unsuitable inquiries. Following that, essential information such as the lead source, the buyer's name, contact details, and their specific market requirements can be carefully reviewed and established.

If the enquiry has come through an online channel, the buyer's basic information should already be in hand. It still pays to contact them by phone to confirm their details. The sooner one-on-one communication is established, the better it is for the seller.

For walk-in or phone enquiries, vital information can be elicited in person.

The seller needs to separate this step from step two, the discovery step. The focus is on making an appointment for the next step rather than launching straight into a Q and A session. In some situations, that's not practical or possible. For example, the enquiry could be very straightforward and inexpensive, or the need could be urgent, so speed is of the essence.

Step 2 – Discovery

The discovery and add value steps are both designed to position buyers towards making a purchase rather than selling to them. They're closely aligned because sometimes, this all needs to happen within a short time period. The term *discovery* refers to a buyer discovery meeting.

From the seller's perspective, discovery is essentially an information-gathering or needs analysis session with preplanned or scripted questions – just don't call it discovery or make it obvious. Sellers use discovery to understand the buyer's needs, find pain points, and discover the actual problem that needs solving.

As many buyers can rarely state exactly what their real needs are, the seller looks to interpret, clarify, and in some instances, influence, their voice.

Step 3 – Add Value

At step three, sellers create an opportunity to set themselves apart by establishing trust and fostering a sense of confidence in the relationship. They can achieve this by employing various strategies, such as sharing helpful information through email or introducing their buyers to knowledgeable colleagues. These colleagues can offer additional insights and explanations regarding any technical or operational aspects that may require further discussion.

At this stage, the seller should be prepared to reveal any unknown needs or pain points they identified during discovery. They can further elaborate on their observations and inquire more deeply to gain a better understanding of the buyer's viewpoint.

By introducing fresh information or distinctive insights at a later point in the process, sellers can positively surprise the buyer and foster the expectation of a superior and innovative solution. Additionally, this approach restricts the buyer's ability to normalise their expertise by offering it to their competitors.

Step 4 – Engage

Step 4 is all about bringing things together and positioning for a baton change from buyer control to seller control. Once the seller is confident they've developed a solution that aligns with the buyer's vision, and addresses their pain points, it's time to engage and reveal their value proposition.

The key to step 4 is to keep everything in either conceptual or draft form. It is a platform for briefing the buyer, taking their feedback, and gathering momentum. Opportunities to trial close may also become apparent.

If the buyer provides positive feedback, the seller may consider expediting the process by transitioning to step 5. They can either inquire if the buyer is in a position to make a decision or request permission to proceed and make the booking. If the buyer responds affirmatively, the final proposal should be promptly sent for signing.

If the buyer raises concerns, provides mixed feedback, or is not ready to decide, this is the ideal moment for the seller to ask additional questions and uncover their reasons. To transition to step 5, the seller expresses gratitude for the buyer's time and confirms that their formal proposal will be prepared and forwarded ASAP or reviewed in light of the feedback received.

Special Note: In certain situations, step 4 may not be possible or feasible. The seller may need to skip that step and present their written proposal without an opportunity to assess the buyer's initial reaction. In such situations, it is recommended to inform the buyer via a text message as soon as the written proposal is on its way. This action ensures it doesn't sit in the buyer's inbox or worse, junk mail folder, and sets the scene for a timely follow-up call.

Step 5 – Commit

If the buyer's feedback was positive, the seller can either finalise their pricing and call the buyer back to close the deal or prepare and forward their formal proposal.

If the buyer's feedback indicated a need to repurpose their approach, the seller is now able to make the necessary adjustments and get their revamped proposal assembled and en route ASAP. Speed is of the essence, as the buyer may view any further delays or tardiness in a negative light.

Even after receiving a verbal or informal acceptance, the job is still not done. It's crucial to follow up and secure a signed contract as quickly as possible. This ensures that nothing falls through and limits the buyer's opportunity to take follow-up calls from other sellers.

Following up on unsigned proposals is the final component of step 5 in the sales process. It's also one of the most important, as there is no sale without a signed contract. If an unsigned proposal or contract lingers in the buyer's inbox for too long, the chances of closing the deal also decrease exponentially.

Key Takeaways

This step-by-step example of a solution sales process serves as a blueprint for aligning your sales approach to the purchasing journey of your buyers. Solution selling is not a rigid, one-size-fits-all approach. It can easily be adapted to suit most sales situations, from single session selling over the phone to making a more complex sale over an extended period.

The key to any sales process is to stay the course and pursue every opportunity to the last step. If you do, you will eliminate your competitors along the journey and consistently find yourself being the last point of contact prior to your buyers making their purchasing decisions.

Chapter Nine:
Know Your Business

For all salespeople, irrespective of their actual role or industry, understanding what business they are in is essential to keeping on track and achieving consistent success.

In today's market, there are a lot of buyers who want the absolute best product or service at the lowest price possible. Through ecommerce platforms, they can also research and source whatever they need, without leaving their armchair.

Having so many options and resources at their fingertips, it's common for buyers to automatically commoditise everything, irrespective of what they are buying. This form of buyer control can sway salespeople away from their purpose. They start selling to the lowest common denominator, or alternatively, attempt to impress and differentiate by overselling.

The first step towards achieving consistent sales success is to know who you are and understand what business you are actually in. There are basically three different categories.

The Commodities Business

If you sell stuff or raw materials, you are in the commodities business. There are two types of commodities, each with subcategories. Soft commodities are divided into agricultural and livestock sectors while hard commodities are either metals or energy.

Commodities are interchangeable, tradeable, and deliverable. A container of beef or a barrel of oil fit the criteria. Another example is the farmer who grows kernels of wheat, then sells them in bulk, by the bushel. The common denominator is that commodities are either traded for investment purposes (e.g., metals) or sold as inputs to produce products or services.

For salespeople, the commodity business can be challenging unless you've attained scalability or identified a market niche. It can be difficult to differentiate yourself, and traditional sales methods built around personalities and hospitality may not be enough to beat off the competition.

Commodity buyers are price sensitive. Luckily, however, not all are solely driven by cost considerations.

If you're unhappy with your current results, the first step to making improvements is to identify what your existing customers are buying and why. To do so, it's important to go directly to the source and solicit feedback from them. Then do some market research on your competitors to discover what their unique selling points are so you can differentiate yourself accordingly.

Here are some ideas for avoiding the price trap as a commodity seller.

- Don't overcomplicate what you are selling. The more bells and whistles you attach, the more costs you need to factor into your pricing.

- Many of today's buyers practice ethical sourcing and are prepared to pay more for it. Things like protecting the welfare of your workers, paying a living wage, having organic certification, and adopting carbon zero business practices can all be key differentiators.

- If you are a longstanding local or family business, position yourself as a heritage brand. Highlight your place in history, the key milestones of your journey, your values, and your reputation. Consumers respect heritage businesses that have survived in the face of big corporate competition. By establishing trust and an emotional connection, you can achieve a major competitive advantage.

- Consider segmenting your product or service offering based on either capacity, risk, or both. If you are capable of delivering higher quality, faster transit times, or guaranteed supply, can you offer these features as premium options that can be separated from your base offering?

- Use your established sales pipeline to market and sell additional products and services to existing customers. You can offer products that are not your own, an example being the electricity sector, which bundles fibre internet services with electricity. This approach allows your potential buyers to purchase essential items in a more convenient, cost-effective, and streamlined manner. By effectively lowering their overall cost of doing business, you can safeguard your own profit margins, resulting in mutually beneficial outcomes.

The Product Business

If you sell tangibles or goods that can be stored, you are in the product business. When a baker purchases a bushel of wheat, it is turned into loaves of bread. These are products. If they can't be sold today, they are stored for tomorrow. If a bushel of wheat costs $10 and is turned into 90 loaves of bread at $4 each, that bushel of wheat has generated $360 in sales revenue.

The primary objective of a product is to satisfy the need for which it was created. A product is tangible; it has specifications that describe its capabilities and limitations. Direct product sales are those that are sold to either a consumer or another business. This could be a person-to-person transaction or through ecommerce platforms like Amazon.com.

When products are sold by retail chains, the retailer is in both the product and services business. While they sell products, they also provide a shopping experience, a range of products from different distributors, the advice of in-house experts, and value-added services that support their product sales. For example, a television could be sold by a retailer at a slightly higher price, purely on the additional benefit of their next-day delivery and installation service.

Here's an example of a motorcycle manufacturer whose products have transcended functionality and created a niche that's the envy of all others.

Harley-Davidson, Inc. is one of the world's most iconic motorcycle brands. Although the company was founded over 100 years ago, the roar of a Harley is still a head-turner today. While their motorcycles are not considered the best priced, best performing, or most technically perfect, they are still considered the gold standard due to their ability to attract buyers and retain them for a lifetime.

> Harley Davidson's secret sauce is in their brand. It's a cult brand that used to mean 'rebel' but now stands for freedom.

The Harley Owners Group (HOG) is a global community of motorcycle owners which is exclusive to Harley owners. There are HOG owner clubs and events worldwide, a company-sponsored museum, customised clothing, and many other tangible benefits. Harley owners are a fraternity, bound together by the HOG lifestyle and the freedom it conveys. If you sell your Harley and buy another brand, you can't be a HOG.

What this example teaches us is that while some products are price-sensitive, there is little difference between selling a product and a service. Harley Davidson's iconic status isn't just about the functionality of their products. In many ways, this is secondary to the sense of community and lifestyle their potential buyers perceive they will experience.

On a more limited basis, the same approach can apply to any product-selling situation. For example, if you are a retailer selling clothes, a new outfit should not only be sold on the quality of the fabric and workmanship, but also on how the buyer will look and feel when they are wearing it.

The seller's approach to product sales shouldn't, therefore, be to automatically pitch their products to buyers. In addition to meeting their practical needs, sellers should identify the emotional gap between where the buyer is today and where they want to be tomorrow. The next step is to suggest solutions and describe the benefits they can expect, both functionally and emotionally.

The Services Business

If you sell intangibles or activities, you are in the services business. For example, if a restaurant purchases 90 loaves of bread from the baker (as per product example) and turns them into 400 entrées at $10 each, they are in the services business. Something that cost $360 is now generating $4,000 in sales revenue.

Like most services, each entrée is made to order, and only becomes a tangible item when there's a client. Selling services is generally less price-sensitive than selling products. The difference is that services are more intangible, and generally can't be evaluated until after they've been experienced. And in some instances, that's not even possible.

Do you need a haircut?

Services businesses are reliant on
reputation and points of difference.

Here's an example of how consumers will pay more based upon the perceived value of the experience, exceeding the ticket price they pay for a service.

Despite the presence of numerous competent hair salons, many of us will pay a premium to have our hair styled by the one person who truly understands our preferences. We place a high value on the personal experience and our anticipation of how the haircut will make us feel, prioritising this over mere functionality. In fact, if our favourite stylist leaves the salon and takes another job, it's likely we will follow them to their new workplace.

The key takeaway here is that being in the services business can be highly unpredictable. One minute you can be the flavour of choice, but in the blink of an eye, your reputation can be tarnished, leading you to be perceived as a product or commodity seller.

All services businesses are reliant on their reputations and points of difference. How customers feel is just as important, if not more so, than their perception of your practical skills. In the above example, the salon lost their most popular stylist and now runs the risk of losing loyal customers and potentially being universally rebranded as an overpriced product seller.

Professional Services

At the upper end of the services spectrum lie those services that are hard to evaluate, even after they've been rendered. The quality of these services is usually assessed based on expectations, trust, or referrals from reputable sources.

Professional services make up most high-end service offerings, ranging from management consultants, accountants, and lawyers to doctors and medical specialists. Professional services are typically paid for through either a flat rate up front, structured progress payments, or billable hours.

Professional services are more difficult for buyers to commoditise due to their expertise and specialisation. In many professions, there's also a statutory requirement to maintain the highest level of ethical and professional standards. However, they are still not immune from competition, hence the need to have a clear identity and reputation for being efficient, trustworthy, and providing personalised attention.

Many professional services providers will choose to diversify so they can reach a broader customer base and don't have all their eggs in one basket. An example of this would be a consulting firm that has a strong internal training focus. At relatively low cost they can use existing resources to establish an external training and development division as an add-on to their existing service offer.

Key Takeaways

It's important for salespeople to always understand what business they are in and avoid being solely judged by price comparisons. Any flavour or element of service you can attach to a commodity or product could be the vital differentiator that attracts more buyers, maintains sales margins, and creates a positive gap between you and your competitors. This can range from ensuring availability and fast delivery times to diversifying your business by bundling additional products or services together.

If you're in the services business, you are reliant on your reputation and points of difference. It is essential to keep your focus on both aspects. If circumstances change or the customer experience is compromised, you run the risk of being commoditised and coming under price pressure.

Chapter Ten:
Speaking Buyer Speak

If you've been reading the tea leaves, you will understand that traditional sales methods no longer work. Your future sales survival (and success) is dependent upon prioritising the needs of your buyers.

For these reasons, successful sales organisations and their sellers have shifted their focus to buyer-led sales processes. In essence, how they make the buyer feel is now as important as the product or service they are selling.

Two concepts that can provide insights into the buyer's mindset are Buyer Think and Buyer Speak. These terms represent two sides of the same coin.

1. Buyer Think

Buyer Think is a term used to reference the thought processes and factors that influence a buyer's decision-making when considering a purchase. This includes their needs, motivations, and evaluation criteria. Most successful salespeople attach great importance to understanding how buyers think and align their sales process to the buyer's purchasing journey. This helps them to make more informed decisions around the design of their sales strategies, processes, and tactics. They are also able to continuously monitor new communication and purchasing trends, so their approach is relevant to today's buyers.

2. Buyer Speak

Buyer Speak is a less commonly known term that refers to the language, communication style, and terminology buyers use when interacting with sellers or making purchasing decisions. Buyer Speak can be articulated in either verbal or written form and incorporate things like the specific words or phrases they use, their tone, and their body language.

Buyer Speak is not one size fits all. It can vary depending on the type of buyer, their personality, culture, and even their emotional state at the time of the interaction. For example, a price-conscious buyer may use language that emphasises practicality, cost, and value, while a luxury-oriented buyer may use language that is more focused on brand reputation, quality, and exclusivity.

Speaking Buyer Speak

The ability to speak Buyer Speak is one of the most powerful sales differentiators you can learn and deploy.

Learning to speak like a buyer will give you a sales edge that your competitors will find difficult to replicate. That's because the majority are only focused on understanding buyers so they can make more sales.

Speaking Buyer Speak is more complex than just adopting the same language they use. It requires a shift in mindset from thinking *about* buyers to thinking *like* them.

The first step towards thinking like a buyer is to ask them open questions so you can dig below the surface and gain a better understanding of their real needs and concerns. Be prepared to challenge their voice, as they may not always state their thoughts clearly, openly, or without their guard up.

By blending their language with your own insights and expertise, you can establish trust and build a powerful connection that will positively separate you from your competitors. Instead of simply repeating what you've been told, your sales solutions will be thoughtful and customised to each buyer's unique situation. That's when you can say you are thinking like a buyer.

> The ability to speak Buyer Speak is one of the most powerful sales differentiators you can learn and deploy.

Getting Started: Learning Buyer Speak

1. Sort out your thinking.

You can initiate the process of thinking like a buyer by reviewing your own attitudes, beliefs, thought processes, and communication style. If you can't 'walk the walk,' then you certainly can't 'talk the talk,' or in this case, effectively learn and deploy Buyer Speak as your communication style.

Self-awareness always starts with taking unbiased feedback. An easy technique is to simply follow up a lost job by calling the buyer and asking them for feedback on your performance. Ask them what you could have done better. Alternatively, have a colleague listen in on your sales conversations and give you some constructive feedback.

As a starting point, here are some of the most common traits and stereotypes buyers find most irritating about the communication style adopted by salespeople.

- Having preconceived notions based upon their appearance, age, gender, ethnicity, social group, etc.

- Constantly acting like they are doing the buyer a favour.

- Listening to respond, not to genuinely understand what they are saying.

- Using jargon and overly complex technical language.

- Being insincere and pushy, or using manipulative tactics to make a sale.

- Being overly persistent and following up too often with little or no reason.

- Failing to follow up on commitments and promises they've made.

- Using a one-size-fits-all approach, with no empathy for their personal circumstances.

- Redirecting conversations to focus on themselves and what they think.

- Being over friendly and personal; failing to respect personal boundaries.

The above list is certainly not all encompassing; however, it does give you an idea of where your improvement areas may lie.

2. Be a servant to the buyer.

As a salesperson, you no doubt understand the importance of being buyer-centric. Unless you work for a company that values the buyer's needs ahead of their own, this can be difficult to put into practice. For starters, most sales teams prioritise short-term gains, revenue, and strike rates over everything else. If revenue targets and bonuses form the basis of your remuneration, it can be difficult to imagine how the adoption of a buyer-led culture will lead to greater financial rewards.

Here are some ideas for how you can improve your sales performance by becoming a servant to your buyers.

- Change your approach from fitting buyers into your structure to understanding what they are trying to achieve and how you can provide solutions that meet their needs.

- Prior to preparing and pitching your proposals, collaborate internally to discuss your buyer's circumstances and identify solutions that can either meet or exceed their expectations while also being operationally realistic.

- Establish the buyer's perfect timing and encourage an internal process that accepts pencil-bookings for a finite time period. This way, you can offer them a guarantee of supply when it best suits their needs.

- If a buyer is contemplating a technical or complex purchase, call upon an in-house expert to explain to them the functionality or usability of your product or service. This advice should be transparent and have no strings attached.

- Be mindful of any biases or disrespectful language that may arise internally when discussing potential buyers and their needs. Make it a high priority to promote an inclusive and respectful culture.

3. Understand buyers' emotions.

During the early stages of your relationship with a buyer, it's crucial to understand their motivations and how solving their problem will impact them emotionally. Keep in mind that most buyers initially approach a purchase with a practical, left-brain mindset. If you allow yourself to adopt the same approach, you will struggle to differentiate yourself, they will stay in control, and you may be exposed to price-based decision-making. For these reasons, you need to understand what drives them emotionally.

While left-brain thinking prioritises functionality, right-brain thinking encompasses creativity, emotion, and intuition. By engaging a buyer's right brain, you can tap into their emotional selves and take them to a place where they feel excited about the possibilities your solution offers. Some of the primary motivators you can uncover to engage a buyer's emotional side and build compelling value propositions include the following.

- Family – This one needs no explanation. For most of us, there is nothing more emotional than how we feel about the special people in our lives.

- Importance – Buyers like to feel important and will favour others who make them feel special. This can be as simple as being addressed by their first name or fitting a service around their needs rather than adopting a cookie-cutter approach.

- Social status – Some buyers feel strongly about their social status and how they are perceived by others. They will align themselves with specific brands and products that not only meet their practical needs, but also elevate their social status.

- Values and beliefs – Many buyers like to support like-minded individuals and businesses that share their values and beliefs. This can include things like a commitment to environmental sustainability and social responsibility.

- Their interests – Sporting, recreational, and leisure pursuits have the potential to serve as strong motivators. This could be anything from supporting a particular sports team to keeping fit or actively participating in a church community.

- Keepsakes and investments – Whether it's a family home, a motor vehicle, antique furniture, or an art collection, many buyers are strongly motivated by the emotional satisfaction and fulfilment they derive from their keepsakes and investments.

Speaking Buyer Speak: Applying the Technique

When it's time to transition from positioning for a sale to actually making the sale, it's time to apply the technique of speaking Buyer Speak. This means putting yourself in the buyer's shoes and either having a finalised solution or testing the waters to gauge their reaction before finalising the sale.

The technique itself is not difficult. It involves acknowledging what's important emotionally to the buyer and doing your research prior to selling them on the benefits of what you're offering.

Here are two versions of a conversation a seller may have with a potential buyer to persuade them to purchase transit insurance coverage when negotiating the collection and delivery of some recently purchased artwork.

Conversation One – *"We have a very good record of getting everything delivered on time and safely. However, as there can be risks, I would recommend you also take out our insurance to protect yourself, just in case there are unexpected damages."*

Conversation One Commentary – This conversation is business-like and practical. It is focused on the seller and their track record of delivering products safely while acknowledging that there is still some risk involved and suggesting insurance as a precaution.

Conversation Two – *"I know how important this artwork is to both you and Judith. That's why I couldn't sleep at night even if there is only the slightest risk of damage in transit. Because of this, I strongly recommend you consider our transit protection plan ... for peace of mind."*

Conversation Two Commentary – This is a classic example of the salesperson speaking Buyer Speak. It shows empathy towards the buyer by focusing on the importance of the artwork to both them and their partner. It conveys a stronger emotional connection and concern for their well-being, rather than just describing the quality of their delivery service and low likelihood of damage in transit. It takes out the word *insurance* and replaces it with *protection*. It is more personalised and has a warmer tone.

Here are two versions of a conversation a seller may have with a potential buyer who is purchasing a television, but specifically, a large screen for watching football, their favourite sport.

Conversation One – *"As we discussed last week, this is the perfect model for watching football. It has a sixty-five-inch screen, wide viewing angle, 4K resolution, good smart features, and high-quality built-in speakers. You can't go wrong with this one, and it's a very good price. As there's generally a fourteen-day delivery period, would you like to go ahead and get things underway?"*

Conversation One Commentary – This conversation focuses on reconfirming and summarising the attributes and functionality of the buyer's preferred television, given the buyer's keen interest in watching football. It emphasizes that it's a good price, which could also be counterproductive and slow down the decision-making process by turning the buyer into a price shopper.

Conversation Two – *"After our meeting last week, I've done some homework and have some exciting news. The season opener is on Saturday night, and I know you'd love to have your friends around to watch it on your new, big screen television. I've reached out to our supplier to confirm we can collect your preferred model from them at short notice and also have pencil-booked a priority installation team for this Saturday morning. If you give me the go-ahead, I can take care of everything, and you can watch the game in style."*

Conversation Two Commentary – The seller is speaking Buyer Speak. The focus is on the buyer's emotions and how they will feel when they are watching the season opener at home with their friends on their brand-new, big screen television. The seller has not only met their practical needs but gone the extra mile to make the seemingly impossible actually happen.

This customised approach takes the buyer beyond their decision to a happy place where everything they need and want comes together. Given the tight timelines, the sale can also be closed under urgency. It's a classic sales situation where both the buyer and seller are winners.

Key Takeaways

Learning to speak Buyer Speak is not something that comes easily to most salespeople. The odds are stacked against them truly understanding the difference between thinking *about* buyers and thinking *like* buyers. The primary reason is simple: sales is a profession dominated by metrics such as strike rates, revenue conversions, and commissions. These benchmarks dictate how performance is evaluated and rewarded, creating a challenging environment where understanding buyers on a deeper level often takes a backseat.

For these reasons, your ability to speak Buyer Speak is one of the most powerful and successful sales differentiators you can learn and deploy. The techniques are simple. The difficult part is cultivating the right mindset. If you take the time to put yourself in the buyer's shoes, build your solutions around their needs, and communicate the benefits in a language that resonates, the rewards will quickly follow.

PART 3

THE SALES CLOSERS PLAYBOOK

From Pitch to Close

The essence of a sales playbook is to provide a reference and learning resource that focuses on the day-to-day practical application of sales strategies and tactics.

True sales success hinges on your ability to effectively apply your knowledge and learnings in real-world situations. The ability to close deals under pressure is the backbone of a successful sales career.

This Sales Closers Playbook is focused on the pointed end of the sales process: the tip of the spear. It is a comprehensive 'learn on the job' guide to everything from building a compelling value proposition right through to pitching, negotiating, and closing the deal. Throughout you will find frameworks, winning tactics, and scripts for nearly every sales situation.

Chapter One:
Sales 101 – Getting Started

Irrespective of your circumstances, personal beliefs, or sales methods, there will come a crucial moment in your sales strategy when the spotlight will be on converting your potential buyers into paying customers.

Being a friendly, genuine salesperson who makes astute observations and creates a good impression is not enough to achieve consistent success. Ultimately, achieving sales success is similar to the distinction between being engaged to be married and actually getting married –what marks the difference is the act of signing a contract to seal the relationship. In sales, that contract represents the ultimate commitment from your buyers to making a purchase. That's when they become customers, and that's when you've closed the sale.

This Sales Closers Playbook is designed to help you capitalise on the positioning and preparation work you have already undertaken by identifying the right approach and timing for closing each individual sale. One of the first things to understand is that sales closing skills are primarily tactical rather than strategic. This is because each buyer possesses unique motivations, needs, preferences, and timelines.

For instance, sticking to a predetermined sales methodology may prove ineffective if your buyer signals they are already prepared to buy from you or urgently require your services. If you fail to promptly close the sale, you could easily dissuade them and open the door for your competitors.

Terminology Refresh

It is common for even experienced salespeople to misuse or misunderstand different terminologies when referring to the same sales actions. This terminology refresh will give you clarity to resolve any confusion surrounding the way these terms are used in the Sales Closers Playbook.

Quotation: Quotations are formal documents prepared by sellers for buyers. They generally contain pricing, contractual details, and other important information, like the seller's terms and conditions. A quotation is typically provided in response to a customer's request for pricing and is focused on facilitating a potential transaction. It is essentially an offer-and-acceptance document.

Value proposition: A value proposition is a statement or set of statements used by salespeople to describe the unique benefits and value of their products and/or services. It is aimed at capturing the imagination and interest of potential buyers and persuading them to choose your solution over the alternatives.

Sales pitch: A sales pitch is a persuasive presentation or conversation where a salesperson highlights the unique value, benefits, and advantages of a buyer choosing their product or services and solution. The salesperson is primarily communicating their value proposition and why it's the best choice.

Call to action: A call to action refers to a concise and compelling message or communication, initiated by a salesperson with the aim of prompting or encouraging the recipient (the buyer) to take a specific action. A call to action can be introduced at any stage of the interaction since its purpose is to guide the buyer towards the desired next step in the sales process. This action can range from scheduling an appointment for the next meeting to directly requesting the buyer proceed and finalise the sale.

Proposal: A proposal is a more advanced or comprehensive form of a quotation. While a quotation typically focuses on pricing details and contractual terms, a proposal goes beyond that to present a more detailed plan, solution, or project scope. A proposal formalises and expands upon a salesperson's value proposition and as such, is the next logical step to closing a sale.

Close: The term *close* refers to the final action of successfully securing a sale or completing a transaction with a buyer. It is the point where the customer makes the decision to purchase the product, service, or solution being offered. It can involve obtaining a verbal or written confirmation of the purchase, signing a contract or agreement, making a payment, or taking any other necessary steps to finalise the transaction.

Trial close: A trial close is a type of call to action that is typically used to test the waters and evaluate whether a buyer is ready and willing to move forward and confirm a purchase. It involves asking a question or making a statement that encourages the buyer to provide feedback or make a decision. Trial close questions are generally closed questions that require a specific answer, usually yes or no. The general rule is that when a salesperson is positioning and gathering information, they ask open questions, and when they flick the switch to sales mode, they start asking closed questions.

Sunset clause: The term *sunset clause* refers to the expiration or termination point for a specific offer which will automatically expire after a certain period of time. The expiry period is determined by the seller and is used to create a sense of urgency and increase the velocity of a buyer's decision-making. A typical scenario is when a salesperson pre-books resources to guarantee that their solution to a buyer's needs is both feasible and achievable. The seller can't hold the booking indefinitely, so the buyer is given a defined time period in which to commit to that opportunity. The sunset clause can also be used to guarantee a specific price and/or secure the availability of goods or services during peak seasons or dynamic trading periods, when supply may be limited.

Pending: The term *pending* is generally used to indicate that something is awaiting a final decision or completion. In the context of sales, a pending quotation or proposal is one that has been sent to a potential buyer and is awaiting their final decision. Even if the buyer has already verbally agreed to move forward with the seller's value proposition, the formal proposal remains in pending status until it's signed. Once that happens, the buyer transitions to becoming a confirmed (and paying) customer.

Single session selling: The term *single session selling* refers to a scenario where the entire sales process occurs in real time, from the initial introduction to the confirmed sale. It can happen through face-to-face interactions or over the telephone, encompassing telesales and customer service situations.

Single session selling can be initiated by either the buyer or the seller, such as a salesperson reaching out to a buyer or the buyer initiating in-person contact. This approach is commonly used for commodities, lower-value products or services, or when there is a clear understanding of the required quantity and a known solution. However, as the complexity of a buyer's needs increases, a single session sales scenario becomes less likely to produce a satisfactory result. It's important to note that in this context, single session selling doesn't encompass click-to-buy and digital sales solutions.

Solid gold closing one-liner: Solid gold closing one-liners are powerful and concise statements that greatly increase your likelihood of closing deals. They have multiple uses and purposes; for example, they can be deployed to create a sense of urgency, reinforce your value proposition, address buyer concerns, negotiate a deal, or ultimately motivate buyers to make positive closing decisions.

It's important to note that not all sales one-liners are effective. Many come across as scripted, artificial, cheesy, or overly salesy, which can actually harm your chances of closing a sale. In contrast, solid gold closing one-liner are tried and tested. When effectively applied they can be instrumental in helping you to consistently achieve successful sales outcomes.

Key Takeaways

Whether you are new to sales, refreshing your sales approach, or a sales trainer looking for fresh material, this sales closers playbook is designed to help you identify and overcome the day-to-day challenges faced by all salespeople. Most importantly, it will help you to boost your closing game!

To avoid confusion, the terminology used for common sales expressions has been explained above. Remember this playbook is not intended to be a one size fits all approach. Don't hesitate to customise it to your needs. If you are in a phone selling environment, you might want to create your own cue cards. For others, you now have some fresh ideas and techniques to incorporate into your existing methodologies and add substance to your existing approach.

Chapter Two:
Build Your Value Proposition

If your emphasis has been on discovering your potential buyer's needs and finding solutions that resonate, you have now gathered ample information to prepare a compelling value proposition. The process of preparing your proposition signifies a shift from a positioning approach to entering full sales mode and driving towards closing the deal. Your focus should be on delivering a clear and compelling outcome for the buyer.

For best effect, your value proposition should include several (or all) of these four elements.

1. An Emotional Trigger

Your value proposition should be built around the buyer's emotions and how the purchase will make them feel. Through the discovery process, you have already identified what a successful outcome entails for them, and now it's time to bring their vision of the future to life. Rather than getting caught up in the complexities of their purchase, shift your focus to their state of happiness and satisfaction. It's essential to recognise that the emotional aspect of the purchase plays a vital role in your sales solution.

2. A Logistics or Operational Component

This is essential to instil complete confidence in the buyer regarding your practical and technical competence. They need to know that you can deliver on their expectation of a trouble- and risk-free service.

When preparing your proposition, a good tip is to establish a project timeline and sequence of events from the buyer's perfect outcome (in the future) back to the present. This should be personalised to their needs. Depending on circumstances, you could also consider pencil-booking (at no obligation) the essential resources to guarantee you can meet those needs. This will add further weight and urgency to your proposition. A key trigger may involve changing their original timeframes to ensure everything comes together on time and as they have described.

3. A Compelling Price vs Value Equation

> Buyers are value extractors and will buy from you when their gains outweigh their pains.

While price-based decision-making will often appear to be the buyer's intention, it's rarely the determining factor. Your job is to sell on value, not price.

Buyers are value extractors and will buy when their gains outweigh their pains.

When comparing products and services, a buyer's purchasing decision will generally come down to this formula.

Perceived Benefits – Perceived Costs = Value

Value is created when perceived benefits exceed perceived costs.

A compelling value proposition should include both tangible and intangible benefits. The tangible benefits are the obvious ones – brand, warranty, capability, price, systems. The intangible benefits are generally emotional ones – your people, responsiveness, comfort, trust, respect, openness, genuineness. Having the ability to understand and meet the buyer's social and emotional needs are just as important as the tangible benefits you have on offer.

If you feel a discount is necessary, it's important to compare the reduced price to your regular rates, not your competitors' prices. This is because simply being cheaper may not be sufficient. There are ways to present a discounted price that both maintain your integrity and enhance the buyer's social status.

For instance, you could offer a special price based on the buyer's affiliation with a larger community, such as being a senior citizen, firefighter, or university student. This approach creates a sense of exclusivity for the buyer, making them feel valued and special. It communicates that while discounting is not typical for your business, you hold a deep respect for their social status and the significance of their community.

Bundle or package deals – Instead of focusing solely on the individual price of your product or service, consider offering bundled packages that provide more value for the price. This can make the overall offer more enticing and demonstrate cost savings.

4. Urgency, Scarcity, and FOMO

Introducing scarcity and/or urgency or the FOMO (fear of missing out) emotion into your value propositions can trigger buyers into making a quick decision. Scarcity implies exclusivity and uniqueness, which can make your offer even more appealing and captivating. It also shifts the focus away from price, as the buyer focuses on the limited availability or time constraint associated with the opportunity.

While it's important to use urgency and scarcity ethically and transparently, these elements can often be built into your overall value proposition as components of the perfect outcome you intend to deliver. For instance, if you have determined that optimal timing for your solution requires you to pre-book or reserve essential resources, you can introduce a sunset clause or time limit for the buyer to make a decision. This guarantees that their booking remains valid as long as they confirm their acceptance within the defined time period.

Key Takeaways

The preparation of your value proposition represents a crucial turning point in the sales process. It marks the baton change from positioning yourself as the ideal solution provider to moving forward and winning the buyer's business.

Your objective is to design a compelling solution that delivers concrete benefits while also resonating on both practical and emotional levels. When taken forward to the next step, this personalised approach will set you apart from the generic pitches of your competitors. This will lead to not only an increased volume of bookings, but also a rise in satisfied customers and the potential for more referral business in the future.

Chapter Three:
The Sales Pitch

Assuming that you have done your preparation and established a clear and compelling value proposition, it's time to pitch for the buyer's business. Your sales pitch should be delivered either in person, on the phone, or over a video call. Unless there's no alternative, it should never be done by email.

The appointment to make your sales pitch should also be separated from your information gathering sessions. Just don't call it a sales pitch when you make the appointment.

> Negative feedback is not a make-or-break moment.

When pitching your value proposition, keep in mind that it is a draft version, not your final proposal. The advantage of staying in draft lies in the fact that the buyer can say yes, but they cannot say no. If you face resistance or receive negative feedback, it is not a make-or-break moment.

Instead, thank the buyer for their feedback and use it to make the necessary adjustments to your final proposal.

To ensure an effective sales pitch, it's important to have a well-structured plan in place. This is because buyers often focus on price, and without a planned approach, it's easy to get trapped into a price-centric conversation and lose focus. Here's a structure you may find useful for effectively pitching your value proposition.

Set the Scene

Start the call (or visit) by introducing yourself, confirming the buyer has time to speak, and upon their affirmation, generate excitement by having a captivating opening. Something like this: *"I've been looking forward to calling you as everything's come together, and I think you will be very happy with what I have to offer."*

Pitch Your Value Proposition

When it comes to pitching your value proposition, there's a method called Whole – Part – Whole. You start with the bigger picture by focusing on the value of your proposition and what it means to the buyer. You then break it down into smaller parts for a deeper understanding of specific benefits before reintegrating these parts back into the whole. You are literally teaching the buyer the value and benefits of your solution.

Here's an outline of how it can work.

Whole – Open your pitch by painting the buyer a history of their desired future and how your solution will make them feel. Communicate with them in Buyer Speak, not Sales Speak.

Here's an example. "*I know that you and your partner are looking forward to a family holiday before you start your new job next month. That's why I've planned to have everything in place before then, so you can enjoy some quality family time with nothing else to worry about.*"

In this example, the focus is on the buyer's family, as nothing brings out our emotions more than our families. This approach sets the table for you to move froward and break down the needs you have identified and your solutions. Before then, don't forget to ask for the buyer's initial impressions and feedback, just to make sure you're on the right track.

Part – Now integrate the vision you have created by filling in the gaps, starting with the timing and logistics of delivering their desired future, from that point back to the present. Follow this with specific features of your proposition and provide explanations to highlight the value and impact of each piece. Remember, you are providing solutions, not trying to make them technical experts.

At regular intervals, pause to take feedback and give the buyer an opportunity to provide input and express their thoughts. This gives you the time to gauge their reaction and if necessary, review and adapt your proposition in real time. At this point, you may wish to introduce some pricing information, including how each component contributes to the overall value and justifies their investment.

Whole (again) – Once you've filled in the gaps, you can bring your proposition back to life by summarising how each component contributes to the bigger picture and their overall well-being. Encourage further interaction and feedback to ensure they feel understood, and you are both on the same page. This is the time to clearly communicate the cost of your solution and emphasise the value it provides compared to the price. Showcase any special offers, discounts, or pricing incentives that may further enhance your proposition.

> Contrast any reduced price you offer to what you normally charge, avoid comparing it to your competitors' prices.

End the pitch of your value proposition with a strong call to action that not only moves you closer to your goal of closing the sale, but also requires the buyer's agreement.

Plan this next step thoughtfully, taking into account the buyer's readiness to purchase and your ability to change their planned pathway. Don't take time out to relax or congratulate yourself; this is the time to accelerate, not slow down.

Depending on the situation, your call to action could involve any of the following: proceeding with the purchase, scheduling a new appointment or demonstration, arranging a call to provide fresh information, formalising the timeline for your firm proposal, or offering a free trial.

Key Takeaways

When delivering your sales pitch to a buyer, you are beathing life into your value proposition, for the first time. Your pitch should be well planned and persuasive, remembering that this is effectively you best opportunity to close the sale, with little or no opposition.

Think of it like this: the purpose of a sales pitch is to float a balloon past the nose of your buyer. In this example the balloon represents your value proposition. If the buyer reaches out and grasps your balloon you've made the sale and just need to formalise the fine detail. If they don't, you now have an opportunity to understand their reasons and refine your final proposal accordingly.

Chapter Four:
Call to Action

When pitching your value proposition, you will have been taking feedback to gauge the buyer's thoughts and feelings. In some instances, they may have introduced new information or highlighted an issue you weren't expecting.

Your call to action will typically serve as the concluding element of the pitch. It is an essential component that guides the buyer's actions and agreement to a desired course of action. The specific nature of your call to action, therefore, is dependent upon the readiness of your buyer to make a favourable purchasing decision.

Here are some examples of calls to action.

1. Permission to Proceed – the gold standard

"Every battle is won before it is fought."

~ Sun Tzu, *The Art of War*

Sun Tzu tells us in his classic book of ancient Chinese military strategy *The Art of War*, "Every battle is won before it is fought." This quote reminds us that success is not just a result of direct confrontation but stems from comprehensive planning, preparation, positioning, and foresight. The easiest route to victory is when the odds are stacked in your favour before the actual battle commences.

If your value proposition has been received with enthusiasm, the feedback has been positive and the buyer's questions answered to their satisfaction, the ideal conclusion to a successful pitch is for either the buyer to give themselves permission to proceed or for you to ask for their permission to proceed and make the booking. If you can achieve this, the sale is effectively closed without you facing any opposition or resistance – reflecting the principle that every battle is won before it is fought.

While this is the gold standard in a call to action, it's important to be attentive to the key signals that indicate the buyer's readiness or their potential to be encouraged to move forward and complete the purchase. Here are some common signals to look for.

Expressing enthusiasm – If they show excitement, provide positive feedback, and express a clear understanding of how your solution benefits them, don't hesitate! Go ahead and ask for their permission to proceed and close the sale.

Asking about next steps – When the buyer asks about the process for moving forward, timelines, or implementation details, there is no reason to delay, as they are actively considering how to proceed with your solution.

Inquiring about pricing and terms – If the buyer appears unconcerned about your price but shows interest in understanding your contractual terms and the fine print, it suggests they are seriously considering your offer.

Discussing specific requirements – If the buyer raises specific requirements related to your solution, they are envisioning how your offering aligns with their needs. If you can quickly and confidently answer these questions and/or adjust your proposition to their satisfaction, that's a sure sign you can move forward.

Expressing a sense of urgency – When the buyer expresses a sense of urgency or you have provided a solution that genuinely creates either urgency or scarcity of supply, this indicates their readiness to make a decision.

2. The Free Trial

The free trial approach invites potential buyers to experience your product or service before purchase. It allows them a test run while still retaining an element of control over their purchasing decision. It is essentially a halfway point between being interested and making a full commitment.

From your perspective, the offer of a free trial is designed to validate your sales pitch and bring the potential buyer closer to making a purchase. This approach is often referred to as "The Puppy Dog Close," as it encourages them to develop an emotional attachment or connection, just as children do when they play with a puppy.

3. Conditional Permission to Proceed

In the conditional permission to proceed scenario, the potential buyer demonstrates a strong preference towards your solution but indicates the need for approval from a third party. Your call to action could involve seeking their permission to proceed, contingent upon obtaining full approval. If they lack the authority to make an independent decision or sign off on the purchase, it is typically because they need to consult with their partner, a close family member, or the person responsible for financial decisions.

A good tactic is to inquire about the availability of the other decision-maker and discuss when they can be reached to secure the necessary approval. Perhaps they are just a phone call away, in which case you can ask when the buyer can contact them, whether it's immediately or within the next half hour. Alternatively, you can suggest the option of discussing it overnight and touching base again that evening or the next morning.

It is crucial to keep the buyer focused and prompt them to act swiftly. If you encounter a genuine buyer who seems hesitant to commit to your proposed course of action, don't be concerned, as they may just want some more time to breathe. You can still successfully close the sales by sending them your proposal and reverting to a more conventional follow-up approach.

4. The Sunset Clause

Just as the sun rises in the morning and sets at night, this offer won't last forever. Don't let the opportunity slip past you in the fading light.

A sunset clause refers to a specific timeframe during which an offer or deal remains valid. Once this time limit expires, the associated benefits of the offer may no longer be available.

When implemented thoughtfully and genuinely, a sunset clause harnesses the power of urgency and scarcity to create a compelling call to action. It urges potential buyers to take prompt action to ensure they don't miss out on a valuable opportunity.

It's important to use urgency and scarcity ethically and authentically. Provide genuine reasons for urgency or scarcity, such as the impact of high seasonal demand within your industry, limited availability of a product or service, time-limited price promotions, or unexpected cancellations that create a late opportunity for your buyer.

Another way to generate urgency is to pencil-book the resources you need to meet specific timeframes, these being essential to delivering your solution to a buyer's needs. Pencil-bookings can't last indefinitely; hence the need to put a specific time limit on the opportunity.

5. Fear of Missing Out (FOMO)

FOMO is a psychological trigger that capitalises on the apprehension potential buyers feel when they believe they might miss a valuable opportunity. The FOMO stems from the possibility that your buyer might miss out on benefits that other members of their social circle or community are entitled to and are currently enjoying. This strategy is commonly deployed to emphasise exclusivity, being another way of creating a sense of urgency and motivating buyers to take action.

The opportunity you are presenting should have limitations and be accessible only to a privileged few or specific social group, for example, military personnel, members of respected community groups, or senior citizens. Don't hesitate to bring to the table case studies and examples that directly reference the positive experiences of their peers who have already benefitted from your offer. By your highlighting the success of others, buyers are more likely to believe they can also experience similar outcomes if they take up your offer.

6. Schedule a Meeting

There are situations where the logical next step after your sales pitch is to schedule another meeting, whether in person, via videoconferencing, or over the phone. This approach is particularly appropriate when new information has emerged during your sales pitch. Instead of attempting to improvise and rewrite your pitch on the spot, it may be better to request permission to reschedule the meeting so you can revise and refresh your value proposition.

Another reason to schedule an additional meeting is if you encounter a complex or technical question. By offering to involve yourself or one of your in-house experts in further discussing specific details and addressing any concerns, you showcase your capabilities beyond mere sales rhetoric. This approach not only demonstrates your expertise, it can also take the buyer beyond their purchasing decision by envisioning you as their chosen supplier.

At the lower end of the scale, scheduling another meeting could be as simple as responding to a buyer's request for more information. While this can be done in person, it can also be appropriate to send an email and/or a link to the information they requested. This would typically be specific information that supports your value proposition and could be anything from connecting them to a database of customer reviews to sending a specification sheet.

7. The Indicative Price

The indicative price is a call to action that should only be deployed in specific sales situations. It is essentially a trial close that can either initiate a negotiation to secure the order or give you the information you require to win the job at the next step, which involves presenting your proposal.

It can be most effective in these situations.

- When you are dealing with a buyer who is fixated on price and will choose the cheapest price possible, if left to their own devices.

- When you have impressed the buyer.

- When the buyer has been underwhelmed by your competitors and delighted to finally meet someone who resonates and talks common sense.

- When you are uncertain of where you stand and don't want to just send out a proposal and hope for the best.

- When the buyer is operating under urgency and needs a price so they can make a quick decision.

Offering an indicative price as a closing tactic requires caution, as some buyers may perceive this approach to be unethical or unprofessional.

The ideal scenario is to be the last salesperson to communicate with a buyer, ideally after they have received competitors' proposals. However, be warned that when they are expecting your final proposal and you call with an indicative price, there can be a period of tension and disappointment. Keeping this in mind, it is advisable to quickly finalise and send your formal proposal immediately following this conversation.

The actual technique for presenting an indicative price is a straightforward one. Here's an example of how you can approach it.

Initiate the Conversation – Start the call with a soft opening, referencing the previous conversation. For example, you can say, *"Last time we spoke, you mentioned you were satisfied with the services I outlined. Is that still the case?"*

Affirmation of Interest – If the buyer confirms their continued interest, proceed to share the indicative price. For instance, you can say, *"I'm calling to inform you that based on our discussions, you can anticipate the price to be around $xxxx. Is that in line with your expectations?"* Depending on their response, you may now be in a position to enter into a price negotiation and close the deal.

Identify New Information or Objections – If the buyer raises objections or provides new information, this presents an opportunity for you to address their objections and if necessary, review and refresh your final proposal at the last minute.

8. Formalise Your Proposal

> The moment a buyer receives your written
> proposal, the control of your sales process
> has also been transferred into their hands.

There are situations where, out of necessity, your primary call to action is to put your proposal together and get it en route. This may be the case when you haven't had an opportunity to pitch for their business, making it the logical next step towards closing the sale. In fact, unless you have received a clear rejection previously, every call to action ultimately leads to formalising your offer by putting it in writing. Some buyers, known as 'spreadsheet buyers,' will ignore your attempts to trial close and instead demand a firm proposal. They earn this nickname due to their preference for maintaining complete control and meticulously evaluating costs, line by line, in comparison to your competitors.

These buyers are classic value extractors and often cherry-pick the least expensive elements from various proposals, aiming to negotiate the lowest possible price for each component. Simply fulfilling their request for a written proposal, especially if you lack confidence in a favourable outcome, can easily result in a lost opportunity.

Key Takeaways

A call to action is a clear and compelling message that is often communicated during or at the conclusion of your sales pitch. In the bigger picture a call to action can also be introduced at any stage of the sales process. It can range from something as simple as scheduling a time for the next meeting to asking a potential buyer to proceed and finalise the sale. As such, there is no one size fits all. The purpose is to prompt and guide your buyers into taking the next logical step, ultimately leading to you securing their business.

Chapter Five:
The Sales Proposal

The sales proposal is a written document you create to formalise and present your product or service offering. Its purpose is to secure the acceptance and agreement of a potential buyer for the purchase. Without offer and acceptance, there is no confirmed sale.

Sales proposals can take various forms, ranging from a simple email quote to a well-structured quotation that includes information on pricing, logistics, and trade terms.

On the more comprehensive side, formal proposals are extensive documents that provide thorough details about the benefits, features, pricing, terms, conditions, and other relevant aspects of the offering.

Each approach serves a purpose. Email or text proposals are typically used for lower-value or informal purposes, while quotations aim to clearly outline the key terms of the sale and ensure the buyer understands the pricing and logistics involved.

Relying solely on a quotation may dilute the essence of your proposal and expose you to being judged solely on price and terms. A well-crafted proposal, on the other hand, is a reflection of your value proposition and contains the key aspect of formalising the offer and acceptance process.

When to Present Your Proposal

Here are some of the situations where putting your formal proposal together and forwarding it to your buyer is the next logical step towards making the sale.

- The buyer has already agreed to purchase from you and the proposal is sent to confirm what you've discussed and get their formal sign-off.

- The buyer has genuine interest in your offer but needs to see it in writing to review the pricing information, key details, any specific requirements you've verbally agreed upon, and assess your terms of trade.

- Your proposition is considered a significant purchase, has a high cost and/or a high degree of complexity. The buyer expects a detailed proposal outlining all the deliverables, pricing, and your terms of trade.

- You've given it your best shot and now there's no alternative but to provide a written proposal so the buyer can compare it to other options and make a decision.

- You've had either limited time or no opportunity to pitch a value proposition to the buyer and this is the only logical step you can take.

- For any number of reasons, the buyer urgently needs your written proposal; if you can't provide it at short notice, you won't be considered.

- The buyer is not the ultimate decision-maker and is representing others who now require everything to be presented in writing.

- You are incredibly busy and there are better opportunities in your pipeline. You need to get your proposal in the buyer's hands so you can keep the opportunity alive while also moving on to the next one.

- The purchase is not considered overly complex or of high value and there's limited opportunity to further differentiate yourself or add value.

Sales Proposal Templates

In most sales roles, it's important to have a variety of templated proposals that cater to different situations, ranging from simple text or email pricing to various types of quotations (based on transaction value and complexity), all the way to formal proposals. Here are the key reasons for minimising free text in your sales proposals and creating a library of templated proposals.

- Time efficiency – Having templates means you don't have to start from scratch for every buyer, giving you more time to tailor your proposal specifically to their needs.

- Consistency – You eliminate grammatical and formatting errors, lengthy diatribes, jargon, spelling mistakes, and other inconsistencies in messaging and branding. You can produce a professionally written sales proposal at short notice, every time.

- Best Practice – The design of your templates can incorporate sections and language that is refined from previously successful proposals and blended with what is considered best practice from other sources.

- Compliance – Many salespeople are nervous about discussing their compliances and terms of trade, as they don't want to put buyers off. Templated proposals provide that essential information, avoiding the potential for downstream issues both with the buyer and within the seller's business.

- Technology – Technology allows you to design and produce proposal templates that eliminate paperwork and can be signed off electronically. There are plenty of options that range from using electronic signature platforms like DocuSign to fully integrated CRM systems. Many have dashboards that can do everything from telling you when your proposal was opened to sending buyers a regular reminder that they haven't responded.

It's important to note that sales templates should still have the flexibility to be customised and tailored to each specific buyer. By making your proposal relevant to each buyer, you will significantly increase your chances of success.

Elements of a Sales Proposal

It's important that your formal sales proposal template has the flexibility to reflect the specific value proposition you have designed for each individual buyer. That's how you differentiate yourself from competitors. Remember that buyers are value extractors, hence the need for a template that reflects what *they* are trying to achieve, not what you want from them. Here are some of the key elements you could consider for a templated sales proposal.

1. Introduction

Begin with a concise and engaging cover letter or introduction that captures the buyer's attention and provides an overview of the proposal. It's important to thank the buyer in your introduction.

2. Executive Summary

The executive summary is a concise overview of the proposal, highlighting the main benefits and outcomes the customer can expect from your product or service.

3. Solution Description

Clearly articulate how your offering addresses the customer's specific needs and challenges. Focus on the unique advantages and benefits that set your solution apart from competitors'. This is particularly important for product sellers, who may wish to insert some technical specifications and their advantages.

4. Special Notes (or Clarity Corner)

This is the text field where you can introduce some creativity by either reinforcing the key points you previously mentioned in your pitch or introducing a unique aspect or call to action that the buyer may not have anticipated. It is advantageous to have a collection of template text examples that you can easily customise and combine.

Within these special notes you should include a succinct and clear message that incorporates at least one of the following.

- An emotional trigger that resonates

- A logistical advantage

- A compelling value/price advantage

- A component of either urgency or scarcity

It's important to use language that resonates with the buyer and to write from their perspective, focusing on their needs and interests rather than those of the seller.

Here's an example of a 'Special Notes' free text field

"At xxxxxxxxx, we greatly value and appreciate the dedication and commitment of our law enforcement community. As a gesture of our appreciation, I am delighted to offer you a special discounted price, resulting in a savings of over $xxxxxx from our regular rate. I know that the correct timing is important to you and your family. As this is a peak time, I have priority-booked your preferred dates, subject to your acceptance. However, please keep in mind that priority bookings cannot be held indefinitely. Therefore, it would be appreciated if you could review this proposal and confirm your acceptance by xxxxxxxx. I look forward to your response and the opportunity to be of service."

This example emphasises both the emotional and practical value the buyer can extract from your proposal. It incorporates a gesture of appreciation for the law enforcement community, a discounted price, a priority booking to signify the buyer's importance, and a sense of scarcity and urgency to accelerate the handshake and alleviate the buyer's fear of missing out (FOMO). In this example, the special community you are promoting is law enforcement.

5. Itemised Pricing

Clearly present your pricing structure and the different packages or options available. Provide transparent information on costs, payment terms, and any discounts or incentives, unless these are covered in another section of your proposal.

6. Terms and Conditions

Specify any terms, conditions, warranties, or guarantees related to the purchase, including return policies and after sale support. A good tip is to keep the buyer focused on the value you can bring by presenting your terms and conditions in an inconspicuous manner, using a drop-down format with a simple tick box on the actual proposal.

7. The Next Step

Clearly state the next steps and what you expect from the buyer, such as the signing of the contract. If the body of your proposal includes a time-limited offer or special incentives, create a sense of urgency by referring back to these.

Key Takeaways

When creating templated sales proposals, it's essential to have a variety of options tailored to different scenarios. These could range from a brief email or rigid quotation format to a more customised, detailed, and persuasive document for complex and higher-value transactions. The common denominator is that your proposal is a document designed to secure the buyer's acceptance of your value proposition.

Chapter Six:
Closing Your Pendings

Once you've sent a sales proposal to a potential buyer, it is now in a pending state, which means it is awaiting a decision or a response from the buyer. Even if the buyer has already agreed to your proposition, they are still in the pending queue until the proposal is formally signed off and put to bed.

The Danger Zone

The period between sending your proposal and securing the signed acceptance is called the danger zone. The reality is that once potential buyers have your proposal, you have transferred the power and control in the relationship to them.

Here are some of the reasons why even if you are the buyer's preferred option, this can still be a danger period.

- Competitor influence – While reviewing your offer, the buyer may continue to shop around, or your competitors may follow up and offer better terms and revised pricing.

- Loss of velocity – As time passes, the law of diminishing intent can take the gloss off the buyer's initial enthusiasm and their urgency surrounding your proposal. If there's a loss of momentum, it can be very difficult to reignite it.

- Multiple decision-makers – The buyer may experience internal decision-making challenges. Other decision-makers may need convincing, want a cheaper price, or become motivated to explore alternative options.

- Changing priorities – The longer the delay, the greater the risk of the buyer's priorities also changing. This can be as simple as taking time out for a planned holiday or facing an unexpected cost that strains their budget.

- Competitive re-evaluation – Once they have all the information, your buyer may decide to reassess their needs, what they're willing to pay, and/or explore alternative solutions.

- Complacent mindset – If you have a complacent mindset after sending your proposal, it's generally because of either overconfidence or inexperience. You are essentially waiting for the buyer to take the initiative and return a signed contract.

- Call reluctance – This is the hesitation or resistance you may sometimes experience before making a timely follow-up call. Overcoming this issue is crucial, as it can be a significant obstacle – and the difference between success and failure.

Getting Organised

As soon as you hit the 'send' button and transfer your proposal from your computer screen to a potential buyer, it will reside in the danger zone until it's signed off. To increase your chances of closing the sale, it is crucial to encourage momentum in the buyer's decision-making process. If you allow the process to stagnate it can lead to a loss of focus and for your follow up calls to be ineffective.

> Send each buyer a personalised text message the moment your proposal is en route.

A hot tip is to send each buyer a personalised text message the moment your proposal is en route. This is an attention grabber that primes them to anticipate its arrival and sets the table for your follow-up call. It can also encourage the buyer to be proactive and contact you with any queries. Text messages are efficient, socially acceptable, and best of all, they have a high open rate.

Here are some pointers to help you organise an effective follow-up system.

Have rules – Whenever possible, do your follow-ups by phone. Establish specific timeframes and rules for when you will perform them. Follow ups are essential but can also be time-consuming, so make sure you schedule sufficient time. Set up automated calendar reminders and alerts to ensure no one is missed.

Prioritise – Prioritise urgent and high-value opportunities and avoid treating every follow-up as being equally important. It's important to be flexible. For example, it's pointless to schedule a follow-up for the following week when the buyer has an urgent need. Resist the temptation to focus on the buyers you like the best and avoiding those you find more challenging.

Use a tracking tool – Use a CRM system or other tools to monitor your follow-up activities, notes, and important dates. In some systems, you can keep track of unopened proposals and set up alerts to remind buyers to review your proposal. If you don't have an automated system, use a spreadsheet or manual files as an alternative.

Document everything – Whether you are using a manual or automated system, it's important to keep a record of your follow-ups and interactions with potential buyers. This helps you stay informed and provides background for the timing and context of your next steps.

Follow-up Preparation

Engaging in prompt follow-ups is a crucial part of the sales process. The best time to follow up a pending proposal is typically within 1–2 days after the proposal has been sent. Finding a balance between allowing the buyer sufficient time to evaluate your proposal and ensuring that the momentum of your sales process is not compromised is crucial.

The objective of a follow-up call is not to confirm receipt of your proposal, it is the next step towards securing the buyer's business.

Always remember that irrespective of any previous interactions, the buyer's full commitment is not secured until a signed order is received. If the situation has taken an unfavourable turn, a well-structured follow-up call presents an opportunity to quickly identify the issue and maintain competitiveness by addressing concerns, revising costs (if necessary), or even negotiating a new deal.

Follow-up Call Structure

Whenever possible, your follow-ups should be by phone rather than email. That's because email follow-ups are generally time-consuming and ineffective.

Before placing the call, take a few moments to sit back and review the details of your proposal, any previous interactions, and the buyer's specific needs. This way, you can enter the call with a clear understanding of your objectives, relevant talking points, and any potential obstacles you might encounter.

To ensure you cover all the essential touch points, here's a framework you can either adopt or adapt for your follow-up calls.

Introduction

Begin the follow-up call by reintroducing yourself to the buyer and expressing appreciation for the opportunity to submit the proposal. Ask if they have had time to review your proposal.

Preferred Seller?

If they have had time to review your proposal and you clearly feel (from previous interactions) or were told that you are their preferred seller, don't hesitate to ask if that is still the case. If their answer is affirmative, now is the time to suggest they proceed to the next step and formalise the booking.

If the buyer validates that you are one of their preferences, but they haven't had a chance to review your proposal, take a few moments to refresh their memory regarding the essential details and inquire if they need any further information or clarification. Should they mention any changes in circumstances or raise minor concerns, you now have an opportunity to adapt your proposal or address those concerns promptly.

Here are two examples that illustrate how you can achieve a positive outcome.

Example One – If the buyer indicates they were surprised by your price, don't be concerned, as they may just be giving you some feedback. Ask if that will prevent them from proceeding. In many instances, they will indicate that it won't. If their answer is that price is a real issue, you may still be in a position to negotiate a reduced price or offer another incentive, subject to their willingness to proceed.

Example Two – If the buyer's timing needs have changed or your proposal has an out-of-date time limit or expired sunset clause, you could guarantee the same benefits for a new or extended timeframe, subject to them formalising the purchase.

Uncover Concerns and Objections

For a standard follow-up where you're unsure of the buyer's preference, move quickly from your introduction to asking the buyer if they have any questions or concerns about your proposal. If they express satisfaction, confidently request their permission to proceed and finalise the purchase.

If the buyer indicates a reluctance to proceed or raises any issues or objections, it's important not to be discouraged. Instead, initiate a conversation by asking open-ended questions to uncover their concerns.

If they make unfavourable comparisons with a competitor, inquire about the specific competitor and if they are comparing apples to apples. Emphasise the overall value your proposal offers both emotionally and practically, highlighting its customised approach to meeting their needs.

When addressing price concerns, underscore the superior long-term value of your solution despite a slightly higher upfront cost. Reinforce the key benefits, such as availability, quality, warranty, and your ability to meet their life needs.

To strengthen your response, you could provide supporting evidence like relevant online customer satisfaction scores. If you successfully address their concerns and are back on track, there is every reason to move forward and ask them to proceed and formalise the purchase.

If price appears to be a significant issue, ask the buyer exactly what you need to achieve to secure their business. It's possible that their requirements are more flexible than anticipated, or you may have included non-essential benefits that can be removed to reduce the price.

If the buyer is impressed with your proposal but feels you are too expensive in comparison to a competitor, consider proposing a compromise by agreeing on a price between the competitor's and your own. Remember to compare the difference between your revised price and your original price instead of directly comparing it to their other option.

Propose the Next Step

Proposing the next step is essentially your next call to action. This could vary from giving the buyer more time to consider your proposal, to getting back to them with more information or closing the deal before the call ends.

If they need more time, inquire about their decision-making timeline so you can plan your next follow-up call immediately prior to their anticipated decision date. If you have received unfavourable feedback, it's important to stay calm and composed, because you still have options available. Rather than leaving it to chance or giving up, there are two approaches you could adopt.

1. You could thank the buyer for their valuable feedback and ask for an opportunity to review your proposal, make the necessary changes, and get back to them.

To ensure you are aligned to their expectations, directly inquire about specific requirements or conditions they consider are essential for securing the order. Ensure you avoid significant delays between this discussion and the timing of your next appointment; the sooner this can occur, the more likelihood of a favourable outcome.

2. If you have the confidence to enter directly into a negotiation, this might be your best opportunity to close the sale. However, before commencing negotiations, inquire if the buyer is ready to make a decision. If they aren't, it may be preferable to ask for more time and make a fresh appointment. If their response is affirmative, this could be your best opportunity to close the sale.

Conclude the follow-up with a sincere expression of gratitude for their time and consideration. Reiterate the next step and your availability to answer any further questions.

Key Takeaways

After submitting your formal proposal to a potential buyer, you enter a critical phase known as the danger zone. During this stage, the power and control in the relationship rests with the buyer.

Even if you've secured a verbal acceptance or are highly confident of a successful outcome, it is still crucial to maintain a proactive follow-up routine for all pending proposals.

Remember, the intention of your follow up call is not to confirm the buyer has received your proposal, it is to understand why your proposal is still pending and subsequently close the sale.

Chapter Seven:
Single Session Selling 101

Single session selling is a term used to describe one-off interactions between a salesperson and a buyer that happen in real time. Whether you're in a busy sales role or handling customer service inquiries, you will regularly be either meeting potential buyers in person, taking sales calls, and/or making outbound calls in response to sales messages.

In many of these situations, you may only have one opportunity to state your case and make the sale. As a result, it's important you have an adaptable single session strategy that combines introductions, information gathering, needs assessment, rapport building, your quotation, sales pitch, and closing into one extended interaction.

Preparedness Tips

Here are some key tips to help ready you for single session sales opportunities.

Be information-ready – Have all necessary information at your fingertips, including pricing details, product/service specifications, timing options, and any promotional offers or incentives. It's a good idea to memorise or have prompts for partially scripted conversations, including standard questions, benefit statements, one-liners for addressing common objections, and trial closing statements.

Practice time management – In single session sales situations, effective time management is essential. Maintain a professional and friendly demeanour while swiftly progressing through your sales process.

Know your stuff – Be familiar with the features and benefits of the products/services you're selling. This knowledge will enable you to confidently address customer enquiries, steer them towards the right options, and communicate the value of your offerings.

Question time – Ensure your key questions are prepared, beginning with simple ones such as confirming the buyer's personal and contact details. Progress to more insightful, open-ended questions aimed at gathering relevant information and understanding their needs.

Be proposal-ready – Have a formal contract or proposal template on hand and ready to get en route and signed off.

Single Session Sales Framework

To help you maintain a consistent sales process, here's a practical and adaptable sales framework you might find beneficial.

Initial Contact

When receiving an inbound sales visit or phone call, it's essential to build rapport quickly in order to create a positive first impression. You can achieve this by introducing yourself and expressing interest in the reason behind their contact.

For example, "*Good morning, my name is James,*" followed by asking, "*how can I assist you today?*" If you don't want to state your name, you could also adopt this type of approach: "*Hello, what brings you to us today?*" This gives the potential buyer an opportunity to share their story and allows you to move seamlessly into your information gathering or follow-up questions.

If the conversation is taking place over the phone, it's important to verify their personal details, such as the correct spelling of their name and their contact information. This helps the buyer become comfortable with you asking the questions and them providing the answers.

When making a phone call in response to a message, you have a better opportunity to personalise the conversation and establish rapport by leveraging the information provided in the message. Once you've introduced yourself, your next step should be to inquire if they are free to speak, and if they have time to engage in a conversation. If they appear to be rushed or distracted, it might be better to suggest a more suitable time for a callback. Making the most of your available time is vital since you potentially have just one opportunity to make the sale.

Information Gathering

> "If everything is to your satisfaction, are
> you in a position to make a decision?"

In a single session sales situation, it's important to quickly transition from the initial introductions into asking your discovery or needs assessment questions. Remember that your questions are investigative tools aimed at gaining an understanding of the buyer's known and unknown needs. Avoid offering comments or opinions until the next step when you formulate and pitch your solution.

Although your specific questions will vary depending on your industry and situation, here are some important ones you could ask.

- *"Can you share with me what prompted you to contact us today?"* This question sets the stage for a meaningful conversation, enabling you to tailor your follow-up questions. You will also discover if they are a returning customer and/or to whom they might be comparing you.

- *"Do you have any previous experience with this type of product/service?"* If the response is in the affirmative, you can establish their previous experience; including did they previously purchase from you, what worked for them, and if they had any issues. It will also lead directly to the next question.

- *"What are the key features you're looking for in your purchase?"* Identifying the buyer's specific requirements, practical needs, and concerns will allow you to align your product or service with their needs. They will generally be calling on past experiences or the experiences of others to provide insight into what functionality best suits them.

- *"What is your ideal timeframe for getting things underway?"* This question is a crucial one. It will establish the buyer's ideal timeline for either initiating and/or taking delivery of your product/service. As a salesperson, scarcity of supply and urgency are two of your best friends. If either exists, the buyer will be operating under time pressure and price becomes less important than availability and supply considerations.

- *"How do you envision this purchase will benefit you in the future?"* The answer to this type of question should form the basis of the solution you will pitch at the next step. It is designed to take them beyond the actual transaction and better understand how a successful purchase will make them feel. Most buyers become truly engaged when their emotions are stirred, being frequently tied to personal elements like their families, social status, security, or financial well-being. Failing to tap into their emotions may lead them to approach the decision solely from a logical standpoint, resorting to a spreadsheet-style purchasing process.

The key question to ask is, *"If everything is to your satisfaction, are you in a position to make a decision?"*

The purpose of this question is to focus the buyer on expediting their decision-making process. As such, it is a question that you deploy strategically, rather than at a specific point in your sales process.

For example, if you sense that the buyer considers you their preferred option, asking this question before your pitch can be an effective trial close, contingent on their approval of your proposal and/or price. In cases of urgency or limited supply, it conveys the importance of making a quick decision to secure supply.

You also have the option of asking this question at a later stage in the sales process, such as using it as a bargaining tool if the buyer expresses interest in negotiating a lower price.

Sales Pitch and Close

In single session sales situations, the buyer's needs will generally be lower in value or of a known quantity and quality. They may have already carried out their research and as such, are well down the track with respect to decision making. What this means is that your sales pitch should be viewed as a point of escalation and kept short and sweet. Here's a 3-part structure for moving seamlessly into pitching your proposal or quotation.

1. Give a brief description of your solution. Focus on how it will make them feel and what it will mean to them once they have purchased from you. For example, if they've mentioned that the purchase is driven by family considerations, focus your pitch on describing how a successful outcome will make their family feel, rather than solely addressing the buyer.

2. Move into the practicalities of the service and/or product you propose. Highlight the specific advantages and benefits of your solution and how it will meet their practical needs while also solving their problem. Discuss their optimal timing and your ability to deliver services within these preferred time limits.

3. Bring your pitch back together by asking the buyer for feedback and whether your proposal meets their needs. If possible, try to respond to any issues or concerns they raise prior to offering your price. When discussing price, highlight any special benefits you have included by way of discounts, limited-time promotions, or special incentives. If the possibility of a supply shortage exists, introduce an element of urgency into their decision-making. Ask if they're happy with your price and if you can proceed and get them booked in.

If they appear positive but want time to think about it or consult with another decision-maker, bring an element of urgency into their thought process. If you are experiencing high demand inform your buyer that while you can guarantee supply in the short term, it would be advisable for them to get back to you promptly, so they don't miss out. they Make sure you follow up if you don't hear from them within a reasonable timeframe.

Handling Price Objections

Be ready for price objections and ensure you have well-prepared answers to manage the most frequently raised ones. Keep in mind that buyers may question the price or inquire if it's the best offer you can provide. In such cases, you should directly ask if your price will prevent them from moving forward with the purchase. Often, they will indicate that the price is not a deal breaker, allowing you to proceed with booking them in.

In other situations, it may be necessary to uncover the underlying reason behind a price objection. Take this opportunity to reaffirm all the details included in your proposal and assure them that you can meet the buyers preferred timing.

If strong price objections persist and there's a notable difference between the buyer's expected price and your proposal, investigate further to understand the underlying reason. If they are comparing your pricing to a competitor's, ask for the exact price difference and reconfirm your proposal's details to ensure a fair comparison. Consider removing any unnecessary benefits that could be sacrificed to lower the price.

If you have room to negotiate on price and are confident of a positive outcome, attempt to reposition your proposal in real time; for example, it may be necessary to offer an additional discount, even if it doesn't match your competitor's price exactly.

If the buyer has a significant price issue (with your proposal) it might be wise to regroup and request time to review your pricing. Schedule a callback appointment and make this callback becomes a high priority, as time is now of the essence.

Managing a Difficult Buyer

While it's important to seamlessly move a potential buyer into your sales process, things may not always go to plan. For example, some buyers may be determined to dominate proceedings and view you as a subordinate rather than a subject matter expert. When these situations occur and things get off to a bad start, it's important to remain calm and let them lead the initial engagement.

If you're meeting in person, try to maintain eye contact, listen carefully, and frequently nod in acknowledgement. If you're on the phone, fill in any gaps in the conversation with positive affirmations. When you have an opportunity to speak, you should recap what you've heard and understood from their statements. By demonstrating attentive listening, you can reposition yourself as a collaborator rather than a salesperson.

At some point, you can assume control by asking thought-provoking questions that challenge their thinking and uncover their real needs. In many instances, this approach will positively surprise and impress the buyer, putting you in a stronger position to win their business.

The Next Step

If the buyer is satisfied with your proposed solution, express gratitude for the opportunity and invite them to proceed with the purchase, guiding them verbally through the formal closing process. This includes getting their dates booked in, preparing a formal proposal or quotation, discussing payment terms, and having the proposal signed off and returned.

As soon as you've forwarded the proposal, promptly notify the buyer via text message, let them know it's en route, and offer further assistance or clarification if needed.

If a signed acceptance is not forthcoming, follow up ASAP to ensure that everything is still progressing smoothly. The timing of your follow up will depend on the situation; it could be within minutes, hours, or the next day, just don't leave it too long.

If the buyer has indicated they are not ready to make an immediate decision or you have no conclusive feedback regarding their intentions, prepare and submit your formal proposal within an appropriate timeframe. Follow the same process of text messaging and following up as described above.

Key Takeaways

Single session selling refers to a sales approach where the entire sales process, from the initial contact with the customer to the final closing of the sale, occurs in a single uninterrupted session or a shortened sales cycle. This approach is typically used when the buyer has a known problem and a known solution or is operating under urgency or time pressure. It is not recommended for complex situations that have a lot of moving parts.

Single selling requires the seller to be highly organised and structured. Right from the first contact time is of the essence so product knowledge, efficiency, and highly skilled rapport building are prerequisites. The use of scripted questions and advanced trial closing techniques can also be highly beneficial.

Chapter Eight:
Price Negotiation Tips and Rules

In a sales role, it's inevitable that you will encounter and address price objections. It comes with the territory. Simply relying on a collection of one-liners to counter price objections is insufficient.

To effectively navigate these challenges and consistently close deals, it's important to have a clear understanding of price negotiation techniques – and non-negotiables. If you rely on intuition or an unstructured approach, you run the risk of undermining your sales efforts by regularly giving ground to the price demands of your buyers.

By adopting a more structured approach, you can confidently steer negotiations, maintain control, and find price solutions that meet both the buyer's expectations and your sales objectives.

Price Negotiation Tips and Rules

Here are ten price negotiation tips and rules to help elevate your price negotiation skills and guarantee better results.

1. Be Prepared to Walk Away

The first rule of any price negotiation is that you must be prepared to walk away from a deal that doesn't work for you. Even if you're in the middle of a sales drought, there will be more buyers around the corner, so don't be fixated on securing a deal at any price. Create an impression that both you and your proposal are unique and the best, whether you're feeling it or not. This will ensure the buyer understands that while you might compromise, you will not make a deal at any price.

2. Don't Negotiate by Email

While sharing key proposal details and pricing with your buyers via email is convenient, conducting price negotiations in this manner is a big no-no. Instead, opt for either face-to-face or phone discussions. In-person communication ensures that misunderstandings can be addressed promptly, questions can be clarified on the spot, and complex ideas can be explained in a more effective manner.

The back-and-forth nature of an in-person discussion enables real-time adjustments and facilitates a deeper understanding of each party's needs and concerns. You also don't have to worry about whether your email has successfully arrived, has been properly read and not ignored, and if it will be responded to. It's a lot easier for a buyer to say no to you by email than either face-to-face or over the phone.

3. Don't Negotiate Without Conditional Agreement

A mutually beneficial negotiation generally occurs when both you and the buyer are conditionally committed to the sale. Savvy buyers often attempt to negotiate before demonstrating their readiness to make a purchase. Engaging in negotiations without securing their commitment puts you at a significant disadvantage.

In such cases, the buyer benefits from your best offer while retaining the option to walk away or apply further pressure for additional concessions. Consequently, you forfeit the key negotiating strategy of give-and-take.

There are also better ways of using your valuable time than negotiating with an uncommitted buyer. To gauge the buyer's mindset and level of commitment, a useful approach is to employ a trial closing question like, *"If we can agree on price, do you intend to proceed with the purchase?"*

4. Aim High, Not Low

When you are involved in a price negotiation, it is generally advisable to start with a higher price than you are prepared to accept. This strategy is known as *anchoring*. Your anchor price is one that gives you the flexibility to lower the price while still achieving a satisfactory outcome. An anchor price is situational, which means that depending on the circumstances, it could be either above or slightly below your usual rate or rack price.

The concept of establishing an anchor price serves as a counterbalance to the tendency of some buyers to propose unreasonably low starting points. You can counter this tactic by gently informing them that their offer falls well below your "approved pricing." This indicates that the value and price you are willing to accept has been carefully considered at a higher level. It subtly communicates that negotiation is still possible, albeit within certain limits.

You will find that many negotiations ultimately become a 'split the difference' exercise, so it's logical to leave some room to reduce your price and have the buyer believe they have won the negotiation.

It's important to note that your anchor price should not be unrealistically high. This can undermine your credibility while also risking that your buyer may lose interest in the negotiation.

5. Let the Buyer Go First

Whenever possible, attempt to enter into a price negotiation by hearing the buyer's price offer first.

Whoever makes the first offer is at a significant disadvantage. If you go first, the buyer is in control of the negotiation and can choose to disregard your offer and request a better price. You don't want to give them two bites at your price before they've even revealed their position.

By having the buyer go first in a price negotiation, you will be amazed at how often their opening bid exceeds either your anchor price or what you are prepared to accept. You can also completely dismiss a low-ball offer and insist that they rethink their expectations. This tactic encourages them to present a second price offer before you even reveal your hand.

By having your buyers present their price offer first, you can maintain control, leverage their position, and increase your chances of achieving a more favourable outcome.

6. *Get the Buyer's Full Shopping List*

> Whenever possible, attempt to enter into a price negotiation by hearing the buyer's price offer first.

Having your buyer's full list of requirements prior to entering into a price negotiation is highly advantageous. This is because their needs will almost always encompass both practical and emotional aspects, with certain requirements impacting the cost more significantly than others.

Having a full understanding of their needs enables you to tailor a solution that includes bundled additional benefits which may hold significant value for the buyer. For instance, their preference for a specific colour or an after-hours delivery may hold great importance to them but have little or no impact on your pricing.

Another reason for knowing exactly what your buyer wants (and needs) before entering into negotiations is to prevent your price from being further eroded by the introduction of further concessions later in the process. While it may not always be feasible to obtain a complete shopping list from the outset, the closer you can get to it, the lower the likelihood of encountering complications as the negotiation progresses.

If you initiate a negotiation without a clear grasp of their needs, there's a strong possibility the buyer may introduce new requirements towards the end, with an expectation of minimal or no increase in price.

7. Don't Allow Cherry-picking

Cherry-picking is often referred to as a weapon of choice for price-conscious buyers. It's a practice where they will meticulously examine each component of your benefits package and attempt to select only those perceived to be priced at the lowest point possible.

This practice, known as *unbundling*, poses a challenge, as the overall value (to the buyer) and the profitability of your offer typically relies on the collective strength of its parts. If you allow a buyer to cherry-pick, you will find that they almost always expect substantial reductions in the value of the entire package. From your perspective, certain components may have minimal costs, but also carry significant value as key elements of the overall proposal.

To effectively combat this tactic, it's important to prevent buyers from taking a piece out of your retail price for the core elements of your proposal. Consider the scenario of a fast-food drive-through. They typically don't provide an option to lower the price of a burger when it is sold as a combo with fries and a drink. If a customer desires only the burger, they will generally be paying a similar price to the bundled package, and occasionally even more.

The mentality of a cherry-picker is that the burger on its own should be significantly lower in price than the bundled package. That's because they can't see value in a full-priced burger without it being bundled into a package with the fries and drink.

8. Look for Variables

As you enter into a price negotiation, it's important to have a clear understanding of the variables or bargaining chips that can be traded. Whether it's perceived or real, a variable is an element that holds value which can be used as either a concession or value-added addition during a price negotiation.

It's important to understand that buyers are generally focusing on the value they can extract from you, without thinking about concessions they could make. That's why you should be looking for variables within their situation as well as your own.

9. Have a Back-up Plan (BATNA)

BATNA is a commonly used sales acronym that stands for the Best Alternative to a Negotiated Agreement. In simple terms, it refers to your Plan B or backup plan in the event your price negotiations veer off track and are unlikely to improve.

> Having a strong BATNA is like an insurance policy; you can say no to a deal because you already have an alternative plan.

When adopted strategically, BATNA is a countermeasure against buyers who are fixated on cherry-picking your proposal, are trying to fit your high-end proposal into their low-end budget, or have a shopping list that includes non-essential components.

In fast-paced environments, pre-planning your BATNA may not always be possible. By asking questions, listening attentively, and thinking on your feet, you can quickly adapt your proposal to better suit the buyer's situation while protecting your own interests. Your alternative plan should be built around making trade-offs that will reduce their overall price while protecting your own interests and margin. In other words, it should be a mutually beneficial situation, not a concession.

10. Keep Accurate Notes

While the importance of keeping accurate notes during a negotiation may seem obvious, its significance cannot be overstated. Your notes play a crucial role in providing recall by capturing specific points, concessions made, and agreed-upon terms. They serve as a reliable reference and can safeguard you against misunderstandings and misinterpretations that arise from relying solely on memory.

Equally important is to ensure that your buyers are aware of your note-taking practice. That's because it's common for them to not remember, or overlook details that are not in their favour, including concessions they may have made. Additionally, they may inadvertently confuse your proposals with those of your competitors, leading to potential misunderstandings.

During prolonged negotiations, it is highly beneficial to commence each new interaction by reviewing your notes. They serve as a helpful reminder to the buyer about the current state of the negotiation while also showcasing that you are highly organised and have a full understanding of where things are.

Overall, keeping accurate notes during a price negotiation helps you maintain accuracy, reference essential details, prepare for future meetings, and build trust with the buyer.

Chapter Nine:
Solid Gold Closing One-Liners

A solid gold one-liner is an impactful statement that grabs attention and conveys a message. Unlike other one-liners, solid gold ones have been tried, tested, and refined for maximum effectiveness.

One-liners can be equally effective in most sales situations. The purpose is the same – to focus the buyer and make it easy for them to buy from you. In a fast-paced sales environment where time is limited, you can use them to quickly grab your buyer's attention and communicate a strong call to action. In a complex situation, they can be deployed to navigate the buyer beyond the complexity of their challenge to a place of clarity and simplicity.

Readiness to Buy

There is no right or wrong time to introduce the most appropriate version of these readiness-to-buy one-liners. The variation you choose will depend on the situation, your communication style, and what you are trying to achieve.

"If everything is to your satisfaction, are you in a position to make a decision?"

"Are you in a position to make a decision?"

In the event your buyer indicates they aren't able to make a decision, then you are perfectly set up to ask your follow-up question.

"Can you tell me what is preventing you from making a decision and moving forward?"

These one-liners can be introduced to filter out time-wasters, uncover additional decision-makers, function as an assumptive close, or prompt immediate action from a buyer who clearly favours your services. They can also be introduced as a simple but effective trial close technique for buyers who appear unfocussed or confused by the complexity of their purchasing decision.

Trial Closing

Trial close one-liners are designed to either close a sale informally, gauge the potential buyer's readiness to proceed, and/or uncover and address any issues or concerns.

Here are four solid gold trial closing one-liners you may find useful.

1. *"Based upon what we've discussed, can I have your permission to proceed and get you booked in?"*

2. *"Based upon today's discussion, can I have your approval to proceed and confirm your booking?"*

3. *"It seems like this is perfect for your needs. If I can guarantee a price of around $xxxx, are you comfortable with moving forward and securing the booking?"*

4. *"Based on everything we've discussed, are you ready to take the next step and move forward with this?"*

Fear of Missing Out (FOMO)

FOMO (fear of missing out) refers to leveraging the fear or anxiety that potential buyers may have about missing a valuable opportunity or deal. By highlighting scarcity, exclusivity, or time-sensitive discounts, you can capitalise on FOMO by encouraging your buyer(s) to take immediate action.

Several of the examples below include the use of a sunset clause. This term refers to a specific time limit during which your offer remains valid. The time limit allowed for your buyer to make a decision should be tight, but reasonable. If the time allowed is too short or too extended, it will generally result in a lost opportunity.

- *"We are experiencing high demand. To avoid missing out, can I please have your permission to proceed and confirm the booking?"*

- *"The special deal I've offered has come about due to a late cancellation. I recommend you move quickly, as it's only available on a first come, first served basis."*

- *"I can only hold this special price until five p.m. on Friday, so could you please confirm your acceptance before then?"*

- *"As time is getting shorter, I've pencil-booked your dates on a priority basis. I can only hold this booking for twenty-four hours so would appreciate you confirming your acceptance by ten o'clock tomorrow morning."*

- *"I'd hate you to miss out on your preferred dates, so will need you to confirm your acceptance by five p.m. tomorrow, as I can't guarantee them beyond then."*

- *"As we are moving into the peak season, I recommend you confirm your booking as soon as possible. This will guarantee availability and lock in the best price."*

- *"I know you and your family will love this purchase. For peace of mind, I recommend you move quickly and confirm the booking, as I don't want you to miss out."*

While each of these one-liners is slightly different, they are all designed to convey a sense of urgency, exclusivity, and the fear of missing out on a valuable opportunity.

Closing One-liners for Follow-ups

If your sales approach has been on genuinely providing your buyer with concrete benefits, and assuming you have presented a compelling value proposition and overcome any obvious objections and resistance points, you have every reason to ask the buyer if they wish to proceed to the next step and make the purchase.

A closing one-liner is typically delivered at the conclusion of the sales process. It serves as the final persuasive statement before the buyer accepts the proposal. For this reason, a number of these one-liners are specific to the follow-up of a pending proposal.

- *"Last time we spoke, you mentioned that our proposal was perfect for your needs. Now you have everything in writing, shall we proceed to the next step?"*

- *"The reason for my call is that I noticed you haven't signed our acceptance form. Can you tell me where you're at, as I'd like to move forward and get everything in place."*

- *"I'm just calling to let you know that since we spoke, we've been experiencing exceedingly high demand. I would hate you to miss out, so can I pencil-book your dates while we firm up the details?"*

- *"Since I sent you our proposal, we've had a late cancellation and I'm excited to report that the exact dates you requested are available. I've held them for you but will need your approval to proceed."*

- *"I'm just following up to see if you've received our proposal. I'm happy to discuss any questions you have and hopefully we can finalise things."*

- *"I'm just touching base regarding the quotation I sent you. Is there anything further I can do to assist you in making a decision?"*

- *"I'm just calling to check in on the quotation I sent you. Is there anything I've missed that could prevent us from finalising arrangements?"*

It's important to remind yourself that these one-liners are designed to close out the sales process. They are the last piece of the puzzle that stand between yourself, the buyer, and a successful sale. Adapt and adjust them to match your personal style, the buyer's personality, and their specific circumstances.

One-liners for Beating Price Objections

As you already know, even when your product or service is the absolute best fit for a potential buyer, there's still a good chance you will encounter a price objection.

Here is a selection of one-liners that will assist you in beating price objections.

- *"You mentioned there is a price difference between my proposal and another you are considering. Can we please review what's included in my proposal to ensure that you're comparing apples to apples?"*

- *"Will this price difference stand in the way of us moving forward?"*

- *"I can assure you that given the quality of our service, this price is extremely competitive. Will our price stand in the way of us working together?"*

- *"This price difference may seem high right now, but I'm sure you will feel it was money well spent when you review your decision further down the track."*

- *"I appreciate your feedback on the price. Can I review this, and do you have a budget range to work towards?"*

- *"I completely understand your price concern. Could we discuss some alternative options that may better suit your budget without compromising on quality and service?"*

- *"With your permission, can I have an opportunity to review my proposal and come back to you with a better deal?"*

- *"The price difference you mentioned is significant. As our services appear similar, can you give me an hour to review my pricing and report back to you?"*

- *"Thank you for the feedback on our price and your kind comments on our service. If I could meet you halfway between our price and the other proposal you're considering, would you be happy to proceed?"*

- *"Thank you for your feedback on our price and the other option you are considering. If I could guarantee to meet that number right now, can we move forward and get you booked in?"*

While these powerful one-liners can sometimes directly lead to a successful sale, it's important to view them as components of your overall negotiation approach rather than in isolation.

Using One-liners Within a Framework

When faced with a buyer who has declined your proposal or raised a price objection, here is a rapid and effective series of steps to address their concerns and transform the situation in your favour.

Step 1 – Uncover the price objection

"Do you mind me asking what's preventing you from accepting our proposal?"

Or, "When you say we are too expensive, do you mind me asking what the exact price difference is and who you are comparing our services to? The reason I ask is that I might be able to explain the reason for that difference."

Step 2 – Refresh the buyer

"*Firstly, can I just reconfirm what's included in our price?*" (Verbally reconfirm your service offer.)

"*Based upon our level of service, is that price difference going to prevent us from proceeding?*" If there's a pause… "*Would you like me to go ahead and get you booked in?*"

Step 3 – Explain the differences

"*Can I ask if you are comparing apples to apples? In other words, does the other proposal include what we have included, or is there something missing that may not be obvious?*" Followed by… "*As an example, does it include [part of your proposal]?*" (Give examples of where you think the differences might be.)

If the buyer is happy with your explanation and the differences you've identified, ask them, "*Would you like me to go ahead and get you booked in?*" Otherwise, proceed to Step 4.

Or, "*If I can include [offer the buyer an additional benefit] into our proposal at no extra cost, would you be happy to proceed?*" Otherwise, proceed to Step 4.

Step 4 – Where do I need to be?

"*Okay, thank you for that. With your permission, can I please take an opportunity to review our proposal and see what we can do?*" If they answer in the affirmative, ask this question, "*Where would our price need to be, given the services we've discussed?*"

Or build a bridge.

"*If I can meet that number halfway, would you be happy to proceed?*"

Or give a guarantee.

"*If I can guarantee to be within $xxxx of that price, can we proceed?*"

Or match the competitor's price.

"*If I can agree to match that number right now, can I get you booked in?*"

If yes...

"*Excellent, that's great news, I'll confirm that right now.*"

Or, "*Excellent, that's great news, I'll review things and get back to you in xxxx minutes.*"

This four-step framework is not a one-size-fits-all approach but is particularly useful in a high-volume, fast-paced environment. It serves as an example of how one-liners can be deployed in a sequential manner to quickly uncover and counter price objections during the follow-up stage of a pending quotation.

Chapter Ten:
Solid Gold Insights

Top performing sales professionals understand that consistent success is a result of dedication and continuous improvement, not mere luck. It's generally down to having a defined process, a solid grasp of sales fundamentals, and possessing the necessary skills and discipline to stay on track and execute your plan.

Here's a selection of quickfire insights, tips, and reminders that can help you on the path to solid gold sales success.

Seek First to Understand	Histories of the Future	Options Aren't Optional
When you meet a new buyer, your objective is to first understand and then to be understood. Ask open and probing questions, then listen to learn, not respond.	Paint your buyers' vivid mental pictures of their desired future and how your solution will make them feel. Anchor their emotions with reason – not vice versa.	Offer buyers a quarter-inch hole, not a selection of drill sizes to choose from. Find the perfect fit. Too many options destroy velocity and invite price comparisons.

Be Effective, not Efficient

Ditch the email and pick up the phone. The phone is a superior communication device for identifying needs, building relationships, and closing deals.

Mirror the A-Sellers

Study and learn from the strategies and tactics of sales winners, then mirror them. When you achieve repeated success in certain situations, mirror yourself.

Strategy Before Tactics

Tactics before strategy is the noise before defeat. Strategy without tactics is the slowest route to victory. Stick to your plan but combine it with agile tactics.

Use Sunset Clauses

Activate buyers through the use of short, time-specific expiry clauses to change their planned pathways. Be genuine. FOMO, urgency, and scarcity are friends.

Win Without a Fight

If you sit by the river long enough, the bodies of your enemies will float past. If you stay in process and do it right, your competitors will slowly eliminate themselves.

Double Your Sales

If it takes one hour to make each sale, shorten it to half an hour and double your revenue. Even if your strike rate reduces 30%, your revenue increases by 40%.

Sell Value, Not Price

Buyers are value extractors. Blend emotion and reason to create value. When perceived benefits exceed perceived costs, value is created and you both win.

Ask the Key Question

Put velocity into your buyer's decision-making by asking this question: *"Under the right circumstances, are you in a position to make a decision?"*

Stick-to-itiveness

This is an informal and fun expression that means stick with it. Go job by job, take each buyer through your sales process and right to the finish line.

Let the Buyer Go First

When negotiating on price, have the buyer go first. They may offer a higher price than you expected, or you can reject their offer and ask them to try again before revealing your price.

Accelerate the Handshake

Flicking the switch from positioning to sales mode is a judgement call. Stay in process but be tactical. Too fast and you risk losing a price war; too slow and you may miss out.

Put Your Ego Away

In the battle of the giant egos, the loser always wins. If your buyer is a know-it-all egotist, don't rise to the challenge. Let them believe they have won the battle while you win their order.

The Danger Zone	Buyers Aren't Customers	Clarity and Simplicity
This is the time period between acceptance and getting your buyer's signed contract. Don't take anything for granted. The longer they stay in this zone, the more danger you are in.	No matter how well you interact, never assume that your buyers are customers. Your job is to turn buyers into customers by having them sign an agreement or a formal contract.	Clarity and simplicity live on the far side of complexity. By eliminating unnecessary noise, you can prepare crystal clear solutions that resonate both emotionally and on a practical level.

In conclusion, these valuable solid gold sales insights are offered in a tipsheet format to support you on your sales journey. Although each tip represents the surface of a more complex topic, they serve as helpful reminders to keep you on track, navigate through daily challenges, and continually learn and grow in your role.